Cybersurveillance in a Post-Snowden World

Carolina Academic Press
Global Papers Series

Edited by
Russell L. Weaver and Steven I. Friedland

Volume I
Recent Developments in Administrative Law and Alternative Dispute Resolution

Volume II
Comparative Perspectives on Freedom of Expression

Volume III
Comparative Perspectives on Administrative Procedure

Volume IV
Privacy in a Digital Age

Volume V
Comparative Perspectives on Remedies

Volume VI
Cybersurveillance in a Post-Snowden World

Cybersurveillance in a Post-Snowden World

Balancing the Fight Against Terrorism Against Fundamental Rights

Global Papers Series
Volume VI

Edited by

Russell L. Weaver
Professor of Law & Distinguished University Scholar
University of Louisville
Louis D. Brandeis School of Law

Steven I. Friedland
Professor of Law & Senior Scholar
Elon University School of Law

Arnaud Raynouard
Professor of Law
Université Paris Dauphine

Duncan Fairgrieve
Professor of Law, British Institute of International & Comparative Law & Associate Professor of Law
Université Paris Dauphine

Carolina Academic Press
Durham, North Carolina

Print ISBN: 978-1-5310-0597-9
Ebook ISBN: 978-1-5310-0598-6

Library of Congress Cataloging-in-Publication Data

Names: Weaver, Russell L., 1952-, editor.
Title: Cybersurveillance in a post-Snowden world : balancing the fight against terrorism against fundamental rights / Edited by Russell L. Weaver, Steven I. Friedland, Arnaud Raynouard, and Duncan Fairgrieve.
Description: Durham, North Carolina : Carolina Academic Press, 2017. | Series: The global papers series ; volume vi
Identifiers: LCCN 2017014441 | ISBN 9781531005979 (alk. paper)
Subjects: LCSH: Electronic surveillance--Law and legislation. | Civil rights. | Terrorism--Prevention.
Classification: LCC K5480 .C93 2017 | DDC 345/.052--dc23
LC record available at https://lccn.loc.gov/2017014441

Carolina Academic Press, LLC
700 Kent Street
Durham, North Carolina 27701
Telephone (919) 489-7486
Fax (919) 493-5668
www.cap-press.com

Printed in the United States of America

Contents

Series Note

The Global Papers Series involves publications of papers by nationally and internationally prominent legal scholars on a variety of important legal topics, including administrative law, freedom of expression, defamation and criminal law. The books in this series present the work of scholars from different nations who bring diverse perspectives to the issues under discussion.

Russell L. Weaver,[1]
Duncan Fairgrieve,[2]
Steven I. Friedland[3]

Introduction: Cybersurveillance Discussion Forum– Balancing the Fight Against Terrorism Against Fundamental Rights

This book consists of "discussion papers" submitted and discussed at the Cybersurveillance Discussion Forum that was held in Paris, France, on June 15–16, 2016, at the Université Paris Dauphine. The event was sponsored by the Université Paris—Dauphine, the Washington & Lee University School of Law, the Emory University School of Law, The University of Alabama School of Law, the Elon University School of Law, and the University of Louisville's Louis D. Brandeis School of Law. The papers covered an array of topics. Nevertheless, a constant theme throughout the papers was the effort to find a balance between the need to combat terrorism, and the societal and individual interests in privacy and freedom from government surveillance. The papers published here examine these issues from French, Spanish, American, Hungarian and British perspectives. The project was hampered by the fact that governments frequently conduct surveillance operations in secrecy so that citizens have little impact or oversight, or even adequate knowledge regarding what their governments are doing.

Ms. Mariette Jones, Senior Lecturer in Law at Middlesex University, submitted an article entitled *Double-Lock or Double-Bind? The Investigatory Powers Bill and Freedom of Expression in the United Kingdom*. In her article, she ex-

1. Professor of Law & Distinguished University Scholar, University of Louisville, Louis D. Brandeis School of Law.

2. Professor of Law, British Institute of International & Comparative Law & Associate Professor of Law, Université Paris Dauphine.

3. Professor of Law & Senior Scholar, Elon University School of Law.

plores the cybersurveillance situation in the UK, noting that Snowden's revelations regarding the US National Security Agency's (NSA) widespread cybersurveillance operation reverberated through the UK, in much the same way that they reverberated through the rest of the world, and presented the British with a similar dilemma regarding the balance between privacy and security. In the article, she examines the Investigatory Powers Bill (IP Bill) that was being considered by Parliament. The IP Bill provides for the interception and monitoring of communications data, as well as for a "double lock" provision which is designed as a "safeguard against abuses and a guarantor of due process," and the bill's provisions for secrecy. The article puts aside the very real privacy concerns raised by the IP Bill, which are being thoroughly examined elsewhere, and focuses instead on the bill's implications for freedom of expression. In the process, she discusses the extensive cybersurveillance operation already in place in the UK. She concludes by noting that the UK has been willing to trade off civil rights in an effort to prevent terrorism, but she wonders whether the absence of major terrorist acts in the UK reveals the effectiveness of the UK's covert and overt surveillance actions.

Professor Duncan Fairgrieve of the British Institute of International and Comparative Law, and Université Paris Dauphine, submitted a joint article (with professors Weaver, Koltay and Friedland) entitled *Cybersurveillance: American, Hungarian and British Perspectives.* In his contribution to this article, Professor Fairgrieve also examines the cybersurveillance situation in the UK. He agrees with Ms. Jones that, like many other nations, Britons were surprised by Edward Snowden's revelations regarding the scope of the NSA's governmental cybersurveillance, as well as by the scope of the UK's own cybersurveillance operation. He notes that the legal response in the UK is complicated by the lack of one single constitutional document, and that common law constraints on executive action have foundered because of the complexity of the pre-existing framework which failed to establish a right to protection for private communications. He then notes that ECtHR case law has held that the collection of communications data and the interception of the contents of communications interferes with Article 8, but the ECtHR has not held that "bulk data collection and analysis, in the absence of suspicion, is not in itself a disproportionate interference with the right to respect for private life." He then examines the statutory authority in the UK for the interception of telecommunications or communications data is provided by the Regulation of Investigatory Powers Act 2000 ("RIPA"). Although it is in principle illegal to intercept communications, or to obtain information about the use made of a telecommunications service without the consent of the user, RIPA provides certain public authorities with the statutory authority to collect and analyze communications. He then discusses the mechanisms by which warrants are issued, and the types of warrants that can be issued.

Professor Fairgrieve notes that the UK has attempted to build various safeguards and oversight procedures into its cybersurveillance mechanisms. For example, the Interception of Communications Commissioner is responsible for reviewing the interception of communications and the acquisition and disclosure of communications data by intelligence agencies, police forces and other public authorities. The IOCC thus holds the public authorities that exercise RIPA powers to account and seeks to improve compliance by means of scrutiny. The Commissioner is a serving or retired judge who reports to the Prime Minister on a half-yearly basis with respect to the carrying out of the Interception of Communications Commissioner's functions. Professor Fairgrieve also discusses the Investigatory Powers Tribunal which was established under RIPA to investigate and determine complaints of unlawful use of interception of communications and gathering of communications data, as well as complaints under Section 7 of the HRA in respect of intelligence or law enforcement agencies. He also focuses on the Five Eyes Partnership (that includes the UK, Australia, Canada, New Zealand, and the USA) which requires judicial authorization for cybersurveillance. Finally, he examines the proposed legislation which imposes a "double lock" system which means that warrants must be issued by the Secretary of State but do not come into force until approved by a Judicial Commissioner (composed of former or serving judges), who review the proposed order. However, as he notes, it is not clear that the "double-lock" provides a suitable safeguard on the exercise of power because the balance of power to authorize weighs too heavily in favor of the executive. Judicial Commissioners are executive-driven and therefore do not have judicial independence.

Professor Russell Weaver of the University of Louisville and Professor Steve Friedland of the Elon University School of Law joined Professor Fairgrieve on the article entitled *Cybersurveillance: American, Hungarian and British Perspectives.* They note that the situation in the U.S. is ironic because, although the United States Constitution was founded based upon a distrust of government, the U.S. National Security Agency (NSA) has been engaged in a massive cybersurveillance operation that was being conducted almost entirely in secret. The article notes that the Fourth Amendment to the United States Constitution, which provides a seeming limitation on the scope of cybersurveillance authority, has proven to be relatively ineffectual in terms of limiting governmental authority. They also note the extent of privacy surveillance.

Professor Andras Koltay, of Pázmány Péter Catholic University Faculty of Law (Hungary), also joined the article entitled *Cybersurveillance: American, Hungarian and British Perspectives.* In his contribution, Professor Koltay examines the Hungarian situation. Hungary is unique in that state protections against governmental intelligence operations were developed only after the collapse of the Communist regime in 1990. However, as with other nations, Hungary began to engage in greater surveillance following the latest emergence of terrorism on the continent. After 2010, Hungary altered its law on the collection of intelligence information. He notes that Article VI (1) of the Fundamental Law provides comprehensive protections for privacy, including the private and family life of individuals, their homes, their social contacts and reputations, and that there is a close relationship between the right to privacy afforded by Article VI (1) of the Fundamental Law and the right to human dignity guaranteed by Article II of the Fundamental Law. He goes on to note that Hungary's Constitutional Court has outlined general criteria governing the means and methods of collecting intelligence information that are acceptable under the democratic rule of law. The broad-ranging rules governing intelligence instruments are set forth in the individual acts governing the bodies authorized to use them, including the Police Act, the Act on the National Security Services, the Act on the Criminal Procedure, the Act on the Public Prosecutor's Office and the Act on the National Tax and Customs Authority.

The Hungarian regulation in effect provides for two different processes for collecting intelligence information: one for *law enforcement purposes* and the other for *purposes other than law enforcement.* Collection of intelligence information for purposes other than law enforcement may be subject to external authorization or it might not be. When authorization is required by law, the authorization must come from a judge or the Minister of Justice. When the government seeks to detect a specific crime, the collection of intelligence information must be authorized by a judge appointed by the Chairman of the Metropolitan Court of Budapest. Other activities, involving the general collection of information, must be authorized by the Minister of Justice. Collection of intelligence information is allowed if the data is required to perform tasks mandated by law that cannot be acquired in other ways. However, it is possible to obtain exceptional authorization under Article 59 of Act on the National Security Services. If the delay caused by the authorization procedure would deprive the Security Services of the chance to detect crime, or uncover evidence in a specific case, the interests of the effective operation of the National Security Service, the General Director of the National Security Service can authorize the collection of intelligence information under Article 56, parallel with the submission of a proposal for the authorization, pending the decision of the Minister of Justice or the judge.

The Hungarian surveillance system was challenged in Constitutional Court Decision No. 323/2013. (VI. 22.), in which the applicants challenged the collection of intelligence information by the counter terrorism body for purposes other than law enforcement, claiming that the challenged provision violated the Fundamental Law because it allows the counter-terrorism bodies to collect intelligence information without ensuring the enforcement of fundamental rights. The Constitutional Court held that the right to the protection of privacy and the right of informational self-determination are not unrestricted fundamental rights. Intrusion on privacy and the use of data can be justified by both law enforcement and national security objectives. In the meanwhile, the individual is required to tolerate the restriction of fundamental rights to the extent the restriction has a legal constitutional basis. In the opinion of the Constitutional Court, national security tasks include a much wider range of activities than just law enforcement tasks, and the country has a legitimate interest in detecting and preventing individuals from committing certain acts even if the individuals may not have committed specific crimes. However, the Parliament's National Security Committee exercises control over the counter-terrorism body's activities, performed through application of the rules set forth in the Act on National Security Services.

Professor Cristina Pauner Chulvi, of the University Jaume I in Castellón (Spain), focuses on the increasing use of drone technology (also known as unmanned aerial vehicles (UAV) or remotely piloted aircraft systems (RPAS)) in society. She argues that, while drones "constitute a promising technology with potential benefits for European industries and citizens," "they are also of concern because of their potential impact on privacy and data protection." In her article, she notes that drones are increasingly being used by both civilians and government as a way to gather information. While she concludes that the benefits of drones are undeniable, she notes that drones have enormous privacy implications because they can employ extremely sophisticated technologies, including "high-power zoom lenses, night vision, infrared, ultraviolet, thermal imaging, and radar technologies, video analytic technology, speakers capable of monitoring personal conversations, distributed video or facial and other soft biometric recognition." These capabilities allow the government "to take aerial photographs with high definition, for monitoring crowds at events such as protests or sporting, hacking WI-FI networks to intercept communications, the identification of criminals or the monitoring of the suspects." She concludes that "the security concept is being interpreted in such a broad sense that it allows national legislation to evade provisions on privacy and data protection," and that there is a need for appropriate limitations on the use of drones for collecting information.

Professor Rosario Serra-Cristóbal, of the University of Valencia, submitted an article entitled *Surveillance on Data and Electronic Communications in the Counter-Terrorism Fight in Spain.* In that article, she seeks to "highlight the necessity to respect both commonly accepted principles governing data processing and the rule of law when monitoring communications and people's data in counter-terrorism," focusing on the 2015 amendments to Spain's cybersurveillance law. She begins by noting that a certain level of surveillance is necessary in the fight against terrorism, and discusses Spain's National Security Act enacted in 2015. However, she goes on to argue that "it is imperative to determine which risks and threats to security, justify restrictions on human rights and under what conditions" because of "the risk of overreacting to terrorism." She concludes that, if we ignore our fundamental rules, then we will lose the war against terrorism.

The paper by Professor Anne Debet of the University of Paris Descartes, entitled *Cybersurveillance by Law Enforcement Authorities After the Digital Rights Judgment: The Impact on French Law*, examines the situation in France. As in other nations, France has limited the right of privacy in an effort to fight terrorism. In the *Digital Rights* case, the European Court invalidated the Digital Rights Directive on human rights grounds, focusing on the right to privacy. In her view, French authorities have been "deaf" in terms of their willingness to take account of the major role being played by the ECJ on human rights matters. She expresses hope that "in the future, the council will also realize the place that should be given to ECJ case law!"

The final article, Professor Olivia Tambou's *Profiling in the General Data Protection Regulation: Progress, But More Improvements Are Needed,* discusses the scope of the European Union's Data Protection Regulation. The article examines the fact that both public authorities and private entities routinely track personal data in order to analyze individual behavior. She then discusses how this tracking has led to profiling and big data analysis. She then analyzes how these activities are analyzed under European law.

Cybersurveillance in a Post-Snowden World

Mariette Jones[1]

Double-Lock or Double-Bind? The Investigatory Powers Bill and Freedom of Expression in the United Kingdom

> 'Double Bind'
>
> A situation in which a person is confronted with two irreconcilable demands or a choice between two undesirable courses of action.
>
> (Oxford Dictionary)

Introduction/Background

The Snowden revelations, uncovering the scale of surveillance by amongst others, the National Security Agency (NSA) in the United States of America and Government Communications Headquarters (GCHQ) in the United Kingdom, continue to reverberate.[2] From then (summer 2013) until now, it can be safely said that international terrorism and its use of modern technology to both plan and execute guerrilla style atrocities such as the recent attacks in Turkey, France and Belgium[3] have changed at a dizzying pace the world in which we live and the context within which governments have to attempt to ensure basic safety for citizens. Against this background national and international attempts to reconcile rapidly evolving mass surveillance capabilities with upholding notions of the rule of law have proven very difficult. The United

1 Senior Lecturer, Department of Law and Politics, Middlesex University.

2. For a concise, interactive synopsis of the impact of surveillance culture, the Snowden leak and the virtual impossibility of avoiding surveillance in modern society, *see* Rory Cellan-Jones, *Who's Watching Me on the Internet?, BBC iWonder* (2016) available at http://www.bbc.co.uk/guides/zyvmhv4, accessed 21 May 2016.

3. See Jon Henley and Kareem Shaheen, *Suicide bombers in Brussels had known links to Paris attacks, The Guardian*, (March 23, 2016).

Kingdom is no exception. The Investigatory Powers Bill (the IP Bill)[4] currently being considered by Parliament and set to be enacted and in force by the end of 2016 is highly controversial.

As with all new legislation in the UK, section 19 of the Human Rights Act 1998 requires the Minister in charge of a Bill to make a statement as to whether or not it is compatible with Convention[5] rights. The Home Office duly published a short document in March 2016 noting that the IP Bill engages three rights, and extensively dealt with the Bill's foreseeable impact on the Article 8 right to privacy.[6] Although it admits that the Bill also engages Article 10, the right to freedom of expression, notably less attention is given to both the Bill's impact on this right and the way in which it proposes to deal with such impact. Similarly campaigners opposing the Bill have mostly rallied around raising privacy concerns.[7]

It is submitted that not according freedom of expression at least equal weight in this debate is unfortunate to say the least, and at most a risky oversight, especially when one considers that very recently a major area of the English common law was completely overhauled because of freedom of expression concerns with the enactment and coming into force of the Defamation Act 2013.

This essay therefore puts aside, for the time being, the privacy concerns raised by the IP Bill, and instead focuses on its implications for freedom of expression. How then, to go about judging the Bill? A useful framework to follow may be a simple Burkean analysis: Any proposed change in laws needs to start by showing, first, that there's a need for change; second, that the proposed change will solve the problem it claims to solve; and third, that the benefits of the change will outweigh its costs.[8] The following discussion proceeds

---

4. The Investigatory Powers Bill 2015, HC Bill 143, perhaps tellingly commonly referred to in the media as 'the Snooper's Charter'. *See* Rowena Mason, Anushka Asthana and Alan Travis, *'Snooper's charter': Theresa May faces calls to improve bill to protect privacy, The Guardian*, (March 15, 2016), accessed April 27, 2016.

5. European Convention of Human Rights.

6. HOME OFFICE, INVESTIGATORY POWERS BILL—EUROPEAN CONVENTION ON HUMAN RIGHTS MEMORANDUM, (March 8, 2016), available at https://www.gov.uk/government/publications/investigatory-powers-bill-overarching-documents (last accessed May 11, 2016).

7. The third right that is engaged is the right to protection of property contained in Article 1 of the First Protocol of the Convention.

8. EDMUND BURKE, REFLECTIONS ON THE REVOLUTION IN FRANCE, WORKS OF EDMUND BURKE, VOLUME 3 OF 12, Kindle Edition 2016. It is submitted that the pragmatism with which Burke sets about relating abstract notions to real life is very useful, especially in the common law. Therefore, at the risk of oversimplifying, Burkean

broadly along these lines, with the first section examining the current state of play in the UK regarding data surveillance and its regulatory framework, the second section taking a closer look at the IP Bill and the third section analysing its likely impact against freedom of expression in the UK. Given the length and range of the Bill, the discussion focuses on metadata and bulk surveillance.

1. The Problem

1.1 Current Surveillance in the UK

Residents and visitors to the UK find themselves subject to some of the most intrusive and extensive surveillance regimes in the world. In fact, it is no exaggeration to say that the Snowden leaks showed that the extent to which the inhabitants of the United Kingdom is already subject to surveillance is truly staggering. Not only are surveillance cameras ubiquitous,[9] the UK also boasts one of the largest DNA databases in the world,[10] and the Don't Spy On Us (DSOU)[11] campaign group highlighted that GCHQ through its 'TEMPORA' programme was routinely and daily intercepting private communications of millions of British residents to the scale of 21 petabytes of data. To put it in context, this translates to the equivalent of downloading the entire British Library 192 times *per day*.[11] The latter large-scale interception enabled GCHQ to construct a huge database of communications data, or metadata. This is significant

---

conservatism in the sense used in this essay simply means the application of the precautionary principle to the legislative sphere.

9. There are estimated to be more than 6 million CCTV cameras active in the UK, with more than 100 000 publicly operated cameras under the supervision of the Office for Surveillance Commissioners. Matthew Weaver interview with Tony Porter, *UK public must wake up to risks of CCTV, says surveillance commissioner, The Guardian,* (January 6 2015).

10. The DNA database currently holds details of some 5,156,268 individuals—HOME OFFICE, NATIONAL DNA DATABASE STATISTICS, Q4 2015 TO 2016, available at https://www.gov.uk/government/statistics/national-dna-database-statistics, (last accessed May 11, 2016).

11. The Don't Spy On Us (DSOU) campaign is a coalition of organisations that defend privacy, freedom of expression and digital rights, and the members of its executive committee are ARTICLE 19, Big Brother Watch, English PEN, Liberty, Open Rights Group and Privacy International. *See* DON'T SPY ON US, REFORMING SURVEILLANCE IN THE UK, (September 2014), Joint publication by ARTICLE 19, Big Brother Watch, English PEN, Liberty, Open Rights Group and Privacy International, available at <https://www.dontspyonus.org.uk/blog/2014/09/19/reforming-surveillance-we-publish-our-policy-paper/ > accessed 11 May 2016, p 1.

12. DSOU p 4.

because the technology on metadata enables the construction of a clear picture about individuals, without having to directly analyse the *content* of their communications. So while significant procedural and other safeguards were in place regarding the monitoring of individual, targeted communications, the position around metadata and bulk communications data was largely without regulation and therefore exploitable, as will become clear below.

1.1.1 Direct Surveillance Not Needed for Picture to Emerge

When the IP Bill's predecessor[13] was debated in early 2000, only a quarter of the UK population was online, whereas now more than 80 per cent are, with the average household owning several internet enabled devices.[14] These devices routinely track details of websites their users visit, their location, who they chat to or text, etc. People's smartphones not only store telephone numbers and addresses, but also personal information about their finances, family members, religious and political views, medical history and so on. With current technology it is possible to use this information to build up comprehensive pictures of individual lives without the need to listen to calls or read emails.[15] Stewart Baker, ex-NSA General Counsel, said, " ... metadata absolutely tells you everything about somebody's life. If you have enough metadata, you don't really need content."[16] More chillingly, the former director of the NSA and the CIA, General Michael Hayden, asserted, "We kill people based on metadata."[17]

It is against this background that reassuring statements from the Office of Surveillance Commissioners (the OSC) need to be read: If one examines the latest report by the OSC, the level of *direct* surveillance in the UK seem reasonable and subject to rigorous oversight. Indeed, the report shows a *decrease* in instances of authorised surveillance.[18] The OSC therefore felt confident enough to reassure the public that its annual statistics show that all such activity that they oversee is accounted for, properly authorised according to set procedures and once undertaken, overseen until cancelled. It went on to point out

---

13. THE REGULATION OF INVESTIGATORY POWERS ACT 2000 ('RIPA').

14. *See* for up to date statistics on internet use in the UK the OFCOM website at http://media.ofcom.org.uk/facts/.

15. DSOU, 16.

15. David Cole, *We Kill People Based on Metadata, New York Review of Books* (May 10, 2014).

17. Ibid.

18. OSC REPORT 2014/2015 p 11–15 dealing with property interference, intrusive surveillance, directed surveillance, and covert human intelligence sources.

that the number of authorisations for these types of covert activity is far less than is sometimes portrayed—but tellingly, it then stated that the seeming 'over-portrayal of surveillance' seems to come from those," ... who continue to confuse these activities with the access to communications data powers (Part 1 of RIPA").[19] As seen above, directed surveillance is not necessary for a complete picture to emerge or for an individual to be accurately profiled—access to metadata is enough. It is precisely this aspect which the IP Bill proposes to place on a legal footing and which is the subject of this discussion.

1.2 Current Legal Landscape

Several key statutes and cases need to be mentioned to place the IP Bill in context. These include the Regulation of Investigatory Powers Act 2000, the EU's Data Retention Directive and the case (*Digital Rights Ireland*) which made short shrift of it, and the UK's response to this in the form of the Data Retention and Investigatory Powers Act 2014. The latter, in turn, was deemed to be not fit for purpose in the UK's "Davis case",[20] with a reference to the CJEU currently under way.[21]

1.2.1 RIPA—the Regulation of Investigatory Powers Act 2000

This Act, which is still in place and therefore forms the bulk of the regulatory framework within which surveillance takes place in the UK, was envisaged to ensure that relevant investigatory powers, including the interception of communications, acquisition of communications data, intrusive and covert surveillance and access to encrypted data are used in accordance with human rights.[22] It has been more than fifteen years since its inception now, which timespan has witnessed the massive expansion of surveillance powers and data analysis capabilities, combined with the rise of social media and advances in communications technology. It is safe to say that nobody still thinks that this Act and the regulatory framework it oversees is fit for purpose—developments have outpaced the law to such an extent that the massive surveillance operations uncovered by the Snowden revelations were by and large legal in the sense that no law was actually breached, mainly because the law itself did not

19. OSC REPORT 2014/2015 p 30 para 5.51.

20. R. (on the application of Davis) v Secretary of State for the Home Department, EWHC 2092 (Admin) [2015].

21. C-698/15–*Davis and Others.*

22. REGULATION OF INVESTIGATORY POWERS ACT 2000, Explanatory Notes, p. 1 par. 3.

envisage the type of data analysis made possible by technological advances. The following example from the operation of this Act suffices to illustrate the kind of loopholes meant in this discussion.

The Act is relatively robust in providing checks and balances for targeted interception in the sense of interception of communications by and to identified persons, but (much) less so when this is not the main route or rationale for the interception. For example, there are strenuous conditions[23] attached to the issuance of an interception warrant in terms of section 8(1)(a) where a single person can be named or identified as the interception subject—but section 8(4) read with (5) largely removes these safeguards if the interception relates to 'external communications', for which a lesser warrant is obtained. In this way, section 8(4) warrants could be (and were, per the Snowden revelations) used as the basis for mass interception by GCHQ of bulk communications data.[24] The Government admitted in May 2014 that it understood 'external communications' to include, for example, social media such as Facebook—so long as the relevant server was outside the UK.[25] In fact, many internal messages and most cloud based communications are routed via other countries, and would thus fall within this understanding of 'external communications'. In addition, regardless of whether communications are internal or external, the Act places no restrictions on the collection of communications data by GCHQ.[27] The result is this: searches directly referencing identified persons (e.g., with the search term 'Jane Doe') are not allowed or at least very difficult

23. Such as the requirement in s. 8(2) that the warrant must comprise one or more schedules setting out the addresses, numbers, apparatus or other factors that are to be used for identifying the communications that may be or are to be intercepted, and the targeted nature of such interception is further developed in s. 8(3) where it is required that this must be limited to communications that are likely to include communications intended to or from the named person.

24. DSOU, 11.

25. Charles Blandford Farr, Director General of the Office for Security and Counter-Terrorism, Witness Statement for the Respondents in *Privacy International and others against the Secretary of State, GCHQ and others,* cases IPT/13/92/CH; IPT/1377/H; IPT/13/204/CH; IPT/13/168-173/H; IPT/13/204/CH (May 16,2014), para 137 and para 138 where the same is repeated for Twitter.

26. Section 16(2) provides: " … intercepted material falls within this subsection so far only as it is selected to be read, looked at or listened to otherwise than according to a factor which—(a) is referable to an individual who is known to be for the time being in the British Islands; and (b) has as its purpose, or one of its purposes, the identification of material contained in communications sent by him, or is intended for him." In other words, only targeted communication falls under the safeguards of ss. 15 and 16 provided in RIPA.

to warrant, whereas searches on the basis of other terms are, as long as the search showed some facet of 'external communications' or comprised bulk communications data—and in this way even though 'Jane Doe' may never have been directly named or searched, a comprehensive picture of her could nevertheless still be formed by analysing such bulk data.

A further loophole exists in the distinction between 'communications', which are strongly protected, and 'communications data', which is not.[27] In the light of current data analysis capabilities, this distinction is arbitrary and useless.

1.2.2 Data Retention Directive

Here the focus needs to shift to the European Union's Data Retention Directive,[28] which mandated EU States' retention of communications data on their entire populations for up to a year in order to combat crime by, inter alia, requiring telephone communications service providers to retain traffic and location data.

1.2.3 Digital Rights Ireland case[29]

The European Court of Justice was asked for a preliminary ruling on the validity of the Directive. The Court held that EU-mandated mass surveillance "entails an interference with the fundamental rights of practically the entire European population"[30] and that the interference was not limited to what was strictly necessary.[31] The blanket retention of communications data as well as the lack of independent judicial decision making about access to data was found to be disproportionate.[32] The CJEU therefore declared the Data Retention Directive not compatible with the Charter of Fundamental Rights of the

---

27. For example, Part 1 of RIPA dealing with the interception of 'communications' require a warrant from the Secretary of State, whereas access to communications data under Part 2 requires only authorisation by a senior member of the relevant public body.

28. DIRECTIVE 2006/24 ON THE RETENTION OF DATA GENERATED OR PROCESSED IN CONNECTION WITH THE PROVISION OF PUBLICLY AVAILABLE ELECTRONIC COMMUNICATIONS SERVICES OR OF PUBLIC COMMUNICATIONS NETWORKS.

29. *Digital Rights Ireland Ltd v Minister for Communications, Marine and Natural Resources and others* (Joined Cases C-293/12, C-594/12), EU:C:2013:845, EU:C:2014:238, [2015] Q.B. 127.

30. *Id.*, at para 56.

31. *Id.*, at para 65.

32. *Id.*, at paras 59 and 62.

European Union Article 7 (the right to respect for family and private life) and Article 8 (the right to protection of personal data).

1.2.4 DRIPA

In response to the Data Retention Directive, the UK fast-tracked emergency legislation in the form of the Data Retention and Investigatory Powers Act 2014 (DRIPA), only for the Act to be declared "inconsistent with European Union Law" shortly after the decision in *Digital Rights Ireland*:

Davis case

In a judicial review jointly pursued by Messrs Davis and Watson (Conservative and Labour Members of Parliament respectively) against the Secretary of State,[33] the high court held DRIPA incompatible with European Union Law as set out in *Digital Rights Ireland*, on the grounds that section 1 of DRIPA is incompatible with Articles 7 and 8 of the Charter of Fundamental Rights, to the extent that it does not restrict the purposes for which communications data may be accessed to serious crime, and access to the data is not made dependent on a prior review by a court or an independent administrative body whose decision limits access to and use of the data to what is strictly necessary for the purpose of attaining the objective pursued.[34]

Rulings by the European Court of Justice (CJEU) in Luxembourg relate to EU regulations and are binding on British courts, although the Home Secretary appealed the *Davis* decision arguing that such decisions are not mandatory as far as domestic legislation is concerned. The Court of Appeal agreed—at the end of 2015 it provisionally set out its disagreement with the Divisional Court's finding above.[35] In a preliminary ruling which raises fundamental issues regarding the relationship between English domestic legislation and European Union law, the Appeal Court expressed the provisional view that the judgment of the Court of Justice in *Digital Rights Ireland* did not lay down, in relation to retained communications data, mandatory requirements of EU law with which national legislation had to comply.[36] The Home Office interprets this as meaning that the CJEU was only concerned with the legality of the EU legislation, and that therefore its findings should not be applied to domestic legislation. The government also argues that domestic access regimes should not be read as

---

33. *R. (on the application of Davis) v Secretary of State for the Home Department*, [2015] EWHC 2092 (Admin).

34. *Id.*, at 114.

35. *Davis and others* EWCA Civ 1185.

36. *Id.*, at H2.

implementing EU law (and as such should not be subject to EU Law and the Charter).[37] This, it is submitted, is disingenuous given that DRIPA was clearly enacted for the very reason of implementing EU law in the UK.[38]

The Court of Appeal has referred questions as to the interpretation of the *Digital Rights Ireland* case to the CJEU (C-698/15—Davis and Others). At present, a ruling is due in this case together with another preliminary reference from Sweden (Tele2).

Whatever the outcome of the CJEU referral and notwithstanding the UK's decision to leave the European Union as per the referendum result of 24 June 2016, DRIPA is subject to a sunset clause of 31 December 2016, so new legislation will have to be enacted.

Summing up: Surveillance and in particular the interception, monitoring and analysis of bulk communications data, takes place against a very fragmented legal background. It is questionable whether existing legislation properly addresses this issue in itself, and to the extent that it does, it is unclear as to whether Convention and Charter rights are adequately addressed. Everyone agrees that this situation needs to be addressed.[39] It is against this background that we turn to the Bill at issue.

2. The Proposed Solution: The Investigatory Powers Bill 2015 (HC Bill 143)

2.1 Overview

The Investigatory Powers Bill (IP Bill) was announced in the Queen's Speech on 27 May 2015[40] and introduced to the House of Commons on 1 March 2016 after its predecessor the Draft Communications Data Bill[41] were

37. HOME OFFICE *op. cit,*. para 111, where the Home Office also goes on to say: "Safeguards in domestic access regimes should be a matter or the domestic courts. The requirements of the Charter do not in any event go beyond the requirements of Article 8, and the provisions of DRIPA are compatible with the Convention."

38. At the time of submitting this article, the United Kingdom have just voted to leave the European Union, further complicating for the foreseeable future the status of EU law and of pronouncements by the CJEU.

39. *See* the comprehensive review of investigatory powers legislation commissioned by Parliament: DAVID ANDERSON QC, *A QUESTION OF TRUST: REPORT OF THE INVESTIGATORY POWERS REVIEW*, (June 2015).

40. HANSARD, HOUSE OF COMMONS Vol. 596 col.32 (May 27, 2015).

41. (London, 2012), Cm.8359.

dealt a death blow by the government's then coalition partners. It aims to provide a new framework to govern the use and oversight of investigatory powers by law enforcement and the security and intelligence services, mainly by changing the existing law relating to the use and oversight of these powers. As already mentioned, the new legislation needs to be in force by 31 December 2016,[42] mainly because DRIPA is subject to a sunset clause by this date. According to the UK Government, the proposed legislation does the following three things:

1. "It brings together all of the powers already available to law enforcement and the security and intelligence agencies to obtain communications and data about communications. It will make these powers and the safeguards that apply to them clear and understandable.
2. It radically overhauls the way these powers are authorised and overseen. It introduces a 'double-lock' for interception warrants, so that, following Secretary of State authorisation, these (and other warrants) cannot come into force until they have been approved by a judge. And it creates a powerful new Investigatory Powers Commissioner to oversee how these powers are used.
3. It ensures powers are fit for the digital age. The bill makes provision for the retention of internet connection records for law enforcement to identify the communications service to which a device has connected. This will restore capabilities that have been lost as a result of changes in the way people communicate."[43]

The Bill itself is certainly long and complex—it comprises 233 sections split in nine parts with a further ten schedules, spanning some 260 pages (the annotated version spans 701 pages). To this should be added six draft codes of practice setting out how powers and obligations will work in practice, adding a further 409 pages of legislation to an already bulky proposed statute.[44] The

---

42. HOME OFFICE, INVESTIGATORY POWERS BILL, Published March 1, 2016, updated March 4, 2016, available at https://www.gov.uk/government/collections/investigatory-powers-bill (last accessed May 9, 2016).

43. The Chapeau to the Bill reads as follows: "Make provision about the interception of communications, equipment interference and the acquisition and retention of communications data, bulk personal datasets and other information; to make provision about the treatment of material held as a result of such interception, equipment interference or acquisition or retention; to establish the Investigatory Powers Commissioner and other Judicial Commissioners and make provision about them and other oversight arrangements."

44. The government published six draft codes of practice setting out how powers and obligations will work in practice. It is envisaged that the codes will be approved by Parlia-

Bill engages the European Convention on Human Rights (ECHR), in particular Article 8 (right to respect for private and family life), Article 10 (freedom of expression) and Article 1 of the First Protocol of the Convention (protection of property).

The proposed legislation has so far been met with ambivalence, to say the least: After largely incorporating comments by the House of Commons Science and Technology Committee, the Intelligence and Security Committee of Parliament and a Joint Committee of both Houses of Parliament, the IP Bill passed its second reading in the House of Commons on 15 March 2016 with 281 votes for and just 15 against,[45] but this must be placed in context: The Labour party (the official opposition) and the Scottish National Party (SNP) abstained from voting, indicating unease with the Bill without at this stage completely blocking its progress through Parliament. What is more, almost 50 Conservative MPs were absent, which may indicate that a large faction in the ruling party may not be satisfied with the Bill as it currently stands.

So, which features of this comprehensive and very large piece of legislation stand out? For present purposes, the provisions regarding the interception and monitoring of communications data need to be examined, as well as the so-called 'double-lock' process which is meant to be its main safeguard against abuses and a guarantor of due process.

2.1.1 The 'Double-Lock' Process

The Bill will provide for an authorisation process under which warrants will be issued by the Secretary of State but will not come into force until approved by a Judicial Commissioner. This 'double-lock' process is much vaunted by the government as a fundamental safeguard to ensure that decisions to issue warrants must be subject to independent judges (called Judicial Commissioners in the Bill.) The double lock process will apply to warrants authorising, among others: interception of communication;[46] targeted equipment interference by the security and intelligence agencies and the Ministry of Defence;[47] bulk

---

ment and will have statutory force. They are the draft codes of practice on: National security notices (19 pages); Interception of communications (101 pages); Security and intelligence agencies' retention and use of bulk personal datasets (38 pages); Equipment interference (83 pages); Communications data (118 pages); and Bulk acquisition (50 pages).

45. HANSARD, HOUSE OF COMMONS Vol. 607 col. 907 (March 15, 2016).

46. Clause 19.

47. Clause 90.

equipment interference;[48] the acquisition of communications data *in bulk*;[49] the obtaining, retaining and examination of bulk personal data by the security and intelligence agencies.[50]

The process is, at first glance, undeniably an improvement on previous uncertainty in that unilateral decisions are made impossible: The decision to issue a warrant must be taken personally by the Secretary of State, based on considerations including whether or not the warrant is necessary and proportionate. The decision then needs to be reviewed and approved by a Judicial Commissioner[51] according to the principles that would apply on judicial review. In this way the government proposes to guarantee that warrants are necessary, proportionate and lawful—i.e., by having a judge involved in assessing them as such. When warrants are to be renewed Judicial Commissioners are to provide the same safeguard.

The double-lock authorisation process was endorsed by the Committees that conducted pre-legislative scrutiny of the Bill.[52] And, in his extensive review of surveillance legislation, David Anderson QC recommended the executive as the primary authoriser with the judicial or independent authoriser controlling executive decisions by applying judicial review principles.[53] It is on this latter point that the double lock process may be criticized because, although in judicial review a judge reviews the lawfulness of a decision or action made by a public body, this is constrained to evaluating the form of the decision making process, rather than the substance of the decision. In other words, judicial reviews are a challenge to the way in which a decision has been made, rather than the rights and wrongs of the conclusion reached.[54] A strong case could be made for the argument that judicial oversight without the power to assess the substance of the government's decision amounts to very little oversight.

2.1.2 Retention of Communications Data

The bill replicates broadly the existing statutory regimes by means of which telecoms operators can be required to retain communications, replacing ss1

48. Clause 138.
49. Clauses 109 and 123.
50. Clause 155.
51. Judicial Commissioners will be former or serving High Court judges.
52. HOME OFFICE, HUMAN RIGHTS MEMORANDUM 2016, *op. cit.*, para 27.
53. DAVID ANDERSON QC, INDEPENDENT REVIEWER OF TERRORISM LEGISLATION, A QUESTION OF TRUST: REPORT OF THE INVESTIGATORY POWERS REVIEW, (Her Majesty's Stationery Office, June 2015), recommendations 84–88, 14.95.
54. JUDICIARY OF THE UNITED KINGDOM, JUDICIAL REVIEW, (May 12, 2016), https://www.judiciary.gov.uk/you-and-the-judiciary/judicial-review/ accessed 15 May 2016.

and 2 of DRIPA and Part 11 of the Anti-Terrorism Crime and Security Act 2001.[55] It also largely replicates the effect of Chapter 2 of Part 1 of RIPA, providing public authorities with the power to acquire communications data, which will include the power to require the retention of Internet Connection Records (ICRs), which are classed as a form of communications data. This largely replicates the problems arising from the *Digital Rights Ireland* case[56] that DRIPA attempted to address, and in the light of the referral of the *Davis* case to the CJEU,[57] remains a problem until clarification is given by that Court.

2.1.3 Bulk Data Collection and Retention

It has already been mentioned how the Snowden leaks revealed that the scope of GCHQ surveillance under TEMPORA,[58] stretched to the interception of millions of private communications and collection of bulk communications data.[59] Perhaps because of technological advances outracing the law, then extant legislation covering the intelligence services (such as the Security Service Act 1989 and the Intelligence Services Act 1994), through their silence on bulk data collection provided loopholes for GCHQ to obtain bulk communications data, as well as private communications of millions of UK residents from foreign partners such as the NSA.[60]

With the IP Bill, the government's response to this seems to be not to condemn or close these loopholes but to give them legal sanction by explicitly building them into new legislation. For example, in its Section 19 statement in terms of the Human Rights Act 1998, the government comments on the Bill's proposed sanction of bulk personal data collection that, "[t]he security and intelligence agencies have existing statutory powers which enable them to acquire and use large datasets containing personal data. The Bill will not create a new power but will create safeguards ..."[61] Professor Joseph Canatacci, the UN Special Rapporteur on Privacy (SRP) quite rightly stated that, '... disproportionate, privacy-intrusive measures such as bulk surveillance and bulk hacking as

55. HOME OFFICE, HUMAN RIGHTS MEMORANDUM 2016, *op. cit.*, p.2.

56. *See* 1.2.1 above.

57. *See* 1.2.2 above.

58. By using warrants for the interception of 'external communications' under section 8(4) RIPA.

59. DSOU, 11.

60. DSOU, 11. See also the Government's Open Response to the claims brought by Liberty and Privacy International before the Investigatory Powers Tribunal in relation to Prism and Tempora, para 194.3.

61. HOME OFFICE, HUMAN RIGHTS MEMORANDUM, 2016 p. 3 para 12.

contemplated in the Investigatory Powers Bill [should] be outlawed rather than legitimised.'[62]

2.1.4 *Secrecy Requirement*

In addition to any consideration about the IP Bill, its secrecy provisions, particularly sections 49 read with 50 should be kept in mind. These are draconian: Not only do they prohibit any information to be published or communicated about any surveillance, surveillance request, data request or warrant, they prohibit in absolute terms any revelation that such a request was made in the first place and they apply automatically to *any* warrant.

2.1.5 *In Summary*

The IP Bill is to be lauded for the 'double-lock' requirement that interception is overseen by judges who need to grant warrants, but it should not be overlooked that in turn, it hands law enforcement agencies more access to individuals' internet connection records than ever before: It requires web and phone companies to store records of websites visited by every citizen for 12 months for access by police, security services and other public bodies. For the first time ever it makes it legally explicit that security services have the power to collect in bulk large volumes of personal communications data, and security services and police have the power to hack into and bug computers and phones and what is more, a new legal obligation is placed on companies to assist in these operations to bypass encryption.[63] Recently in the US, the government backed down over forcing tech giant Apple to unlock a terrorist's iPhone—under the IP Bill, if the same scenario plays out in the UK, Apple would be under a legal obligation to comply with such a request.[64]

---

62. JOSEPH A. CANATACI, REPORT OF THE SPECIAL RAPPORTEUR ON THE RIGHT TO PRIVACY, (UN Human Rights Council, March 8, 2016) A/HRC/31/64, p 14.

63. Alan Travis, *Investigatory powers bill: the key points, The Guardian*, (Nov 4, 2015), available at https://www.theguardian.com/world/2015/nov/04/investigatory-powers-bill-the-key-points (last accessed June 27, 2016).

64. Devlin Barrett and Daisuke Wakabayashi, *FBI Opens San Bernardino Shooter's iPhone; U.S. Drops Demand on Apple—Move delays a high-stakes showdown between Washington, Silicon Valley, The Wall Street Journal*, (March 28, 2016), available at http://www.wsj.com/articles/fbi-unlocks-terrorists-iphone-without-apples-help-1459202353 (accessed 16 May 2016). See also Richard Yorke, *Silencing the Canary: the lawfulness of the U.K. Investigatory Powers Bill's secrecy provisions under the ECHR, EJIL: Talk!* Blog of the European Journal of International Law (May 17, 2016), available at http://www.ejiltalk.org/silencing-the-canary-the-lawfulness-of-the-u-k-investigatory-powers-bills-secrecy-provisions-under-the-echr/ (accessed 17 May 2016).

2.2 Arguments for and against the IP Bill

GCHQ and the Government backers of the Bill argue that bulk interception is necessary as a first step in the process of fighting terrorism and crime. Nobody disagrees that the sophisticated and unique modern iterations of both terrorism and organised crime necessitate a strong response.[65] The way in which this is done is of course contentious. GCHQ argues that the necessary second step is a targeted search of this data carried out under legal warrants and this means, according to them, that the vast majority of intercepted material is never read. A problem with this line of thinking is of course that even if the majority of data is indeed not read, the mere fact of authorising bulk interception legitimises mass surveillance.[66] Furthermore, as was pointed out earlier, data could be analysed to a remarkably precise degree without having to be read, as such.

The complex and controversial bill has, for this and other reasons, been the subject of fierce opposition and criticism, including two hundred leading lawyers representing the legal profession and forty UK law schools, as well as the United Nations Special Rapporteur on privacy.[67] A short scrutiny of changes suggested by the Labour party highlight some of the more obvious shortcomings of the Bill:

- "A clear definition of protecting 'national security' and 'economic wellbeing', which are the current conditions that justify the use of the new powers;
- A proportionate list of crimes that would justify allowing police and security services to access someone's internet connection record;

---

65. *See* the parliamentary debate around the second reading of the Bill, in which all participants accepted the need to update existing laws dealing with surveillance targeting terrorism and crime—HANSARD, HC (March 15,2016) Vol. 607 col. 810—907. For example: Labour's Andy Burnham said during the Bill's second debate that he was persuaded that the police and security services were losing the race against criminals because of advances in technology and that the law therefore needed to be updated to give a 'clear legal framework for access to some internet records. *See* also Rowena Mason, Anushka Asthana and Alan Travis, *'Snooper's charter': Theresa May faces calls to improve bill to protect privacy, The Guardian* (March 15, 2016), available at https://www.theguardian.com/world/2016/mar/15/delay-investigatory-powers-bill-scrutiny-mps-second-reading-firms-campaigners (last accessed June 27, 2016).

66. CANNATACI, *op. cit.*, p 14. *See* also Owen Bowcott, Legal Affairs Correspondent, "Investigatory powers bill not fit for purpose, say 200 senior lawyers" *The Guardian* (March 14, 2016), available at https://www.theguardian.com/world/2016/mar/14/investigatory-powers-bill-not-fit-for-purpose-say-200-senior-lawyers (last accessed June 27, 2016).

67. Ibid.

- Restrictions on the number of law enforcement agencies that would be allowed to use the legislation;
- Better protections for the confidential communications of 'sensitive professions' such as MPs with constitutents, lawyers with clients and journalists with sources;
- Approval for interception to be granted by judges on the basis of the evidence rather than merely whether the right process has been followed."[68]

3. Cost-Benefit Analysis

The focus now needs to turn to the third part of this analysis, judging the likelihood of the proposed legislative reform achieving its stated aims (such as prevention of terrorist atrocities) against its likely impacts, in this instance on freedom of expression in the UK.

3.1 Why Protect Freedom of Expression?

Western philosophy recognised freedom of speech long before its inclusion in the 1948 Human Rights Declaration: Mill's classic essay 'Of the Liberty of Thought and Discussion', dating back to 1859, has proven to be an enduring starting point on the topic.[69] Today freedom of expression is one of the most highly valued human rights, with almost universal acceptance as a *sine qua non* for democratic societies. To name but a few: the Universal Declaration of Human Rights recognises this right in Article 19, the European Convention of Human Rights (ECHR) recognises it in Article 10 (Freedom of Expression)[70] and the Charter of Fundamental Rights of the European Union (the EU Char-

---

68. *See* Rowena Mason, Anushka Asthana and Alan Travis, *op. cit.*(n. 64).

69. JOHN STUART MILL, ON LIBERTY (London: Longman, Roberts & Green, 1869, originally published 1859).

70. Article 10 reads as follows: 1. Everyone has the right to freedom of expression. This right shall include freedom to hold opinions and to receive and impart information and ideas without interference by public authority and regardless of frontiers. This Article shall not prevent States from requiring the licensing of broadcasting, television or cinema enterprises. 2. The exercise of these freedoms, since it carries with it duties and responsibilities, may be subject to such formalities, conditions, restrictions or penalties as are prescribed by law and are necessary in a democratic society, in the interests of national security, territorial integrity or public safety, for the prevention of disorder or crime, for the protection of health or morals, for the protection of the reputation or rights of others, for preventing the disclosure of information received in confidence, or for maintaining the authority and impartiality of the judiciary.

ter) recognises in Article 11 the right to freedom of expression and information.[71] Free speech is therefore undeniably an established right. But every now and again, especially when faced with a situation where it may be affected, for example by proposed legislation such as the IP Bill, it is a good idea to take a step back and re-examine the reasons why it is deemed necessary to protect free speech. Only in such manner can the interests served by this right be judged against the interests served by the proposed infringing measure, and a proper balance sought.

Eric Barendt in his seminal work *Freedom of Speech* provides a clear and concise summary and analysis of the overarching reasons for protection this right.[72] In essence, there are four almost universally recognised arguments in favour of a Free Speech Principle: The argument concerning the importance of discovering truth; Free speech as an aspect of self-fulfilment; The argument from citizen participation in a democracy; and Suspicion of government. It is immediately evident that if freedom of expression is indeed impacted negatively by the IP Bill, all four arguments may be engaged. The four arguments feed into the protection of the following interests: The speaker's interest in communicating ideas and information; The audience's interest in receiving ideas and information; and the bystanders' (or public) interest in speech.[73] Of course the right to freedom of expression is not absolute and needs to be balanced against other values. For example, hate speech must be curbed in order to protect the right to human dignity. Nevertheless free speech is important enough to be granted constitutional protection. In cases where free speech become constrained, we now commonly speak of the 'chilling effect'.

It is recognised that the State poses actual dangers with regard to freedom of speech, albeit in their modern iteration radically different from even a few decades ago. Koltay,[74] for instance, points out that the possibility of *direct* lim-

71. Article 11 states: 1. Everyone has the right to freedom of expression. This right shall include freedom to hold opinions and to receive and impart information and ideas without interference by public authority and regardless of frontiers. 2. The freedom and pluralism of the media shall be respected.

72. ERIC BARENDT, FREEDOM OF SPEECH (2nd edn OUP, Oxford 2005), chapter 1 ('Why Protect Free Speech?'). See also on this topic DARIO MILO, DEFAMATION AND FREEDOM OF SPEECH (OUP, Oxford 2000), chapter 3 ('Freedom of Expression and Freedom of the Media) and in general, RONALD DWORKIN, FREEDOM'S LAW (OUP, New York 1996) and ANDRÁS KOLTAY, FREEDOM OF SPEECH: THE UNREACHABLE MIRAGE (Budapest: CompLex Publisher Ltd., 2013).

73. *Ibid.*, 23–29.

74. KOLTAY, *op cit.*,92–96.

itation of freedom of speech by the State is today severely restrained and circumscribed by constitutional guarantees and judicial precedent. However, indirect action by the State may nevertheless serve to constrain freedom of speech: To take but one example, deregulation of the media (or other areas of civic life), in effect transfers control of public discourse to powerful private interests, thus undermining the very raison d'être of a free and independent press to further a free and frank exchange of a variety of views. Similarly in our analysis the proposed legislation, once enacted and once its implications become clear to the public, may transform public discourse by skewing the free and frank exchange of ideas and information.

Wright rightly highlights the view that abuse of mass surveillance may be inimical to democracy as it erodes the trust between government and the governed and the civic sphere: 'There is no such thing as benign surveillance. It always comes with costs because of the chill it visits on conduct, education, associations, and expression'.[75] We therefore need to examine the chilling effect in terms of its effect on state action and its standing as a concept recognised in law in the UK and Europe.

3.2 Existing Concern about Chilling Effect

3.2.1 The Chilling Effect in European Court of Human Rights Jurisprudence

It has been noted that the ECtHR often remarks that certain measures and sanctions interfering with the right to freedom of expression have a "chilling effect".[76] Although mention of the chilling effect is not limited to freedom of expression jurisprudence under art.10, it arises in that context the most. Furthermore, it has been applied in relation to a variety of state interferences, including for example abortion laws,[77] and interferences with the right of individual petition under art.34.[78] One scholar reckoned that the phrase had been mentioned in over 100 judgments up to 2013, so it is surprising that at the same time there has been a notable absence of scholarly attention to the judicial significance of this chilling effect principle.[79]

---

75. *See* ANDREW MCCANSE WRIGHT, CIVIL SOCIETY AND CYBERSURVEILLANCE (June 24, 2016), 1, 3. Available at SSRN: http://ssrn.com/abstract=2800200.

76. *See* Ronan O Fathaigh, *Article 10 and the chilling effect principle* E.H.R.L.R. 304 (2013).

77. *See* e.g. *Tysiaç v Poland* 45 E.H.R.R. 42 (2007) at [116]; and *A v Ireland* 53 E.H.R.R. 13 (2011) at [178].

78. *See* e.g. *McShane v United Kingdom* 35 E.H.R.R. 23 (2002)at [151], and *Colibaba v Moldova* 49 E.H.R.R. 44 (2009)at [68].

79. O Fathaigh, *op. cit.*, 304.

In essence, the ECtHR jurisprudence seem to indicate that only a narrow margin should be allowed to a state when the restriction of free speech concerns political speech or is likely to discourage people from making criticisms or contributing to public discussion of issues affecting the life of the community.[80] Two remarks may be made here: A vote to leave the European Union does not affect, without more, the UK's relationship with the European Court of Human Rights and its jurisprudence and therefore until such time as (and if) the UK ends this relationship, the ECHR and the decisions by the ECtHR will continue to play an important part in domestic jurisprudence. Secondly, the ECtHR's jurisprudence relevant to the IP Bill's likely impact on freedom of expression unfortunately seems to have fallen by the wayside—at least as far as the discussion of the proposed legislation is concerned. Anecdotally, for instance, the author counted in the May 2016 Parliamentary debate of the IP Bill,[81] more than a hundred mentions of the word 'privacy' by MPs representing the full range of British political parties whereas in the same debate 'freedom of speech' was mentioned twice, and 'freedom of expression' once only.[82]

Furthermore, the ECtHR has also clearly ruled in *Vereniging Weekblad Bluf! V Netherlands* that legislation that prohibits the dissemination of national security information which eliminates public control over intelligence services' activities, in absolute and unconditional terms, constitutes a breach of art. 10 as it goes beyond what is necessary in a democratic society.[83] It could be argued that requiring telecoms operators to retain and hand over to the government bulk data, combined with the secrecy requirement fall foul of the *Vereniging Weekblad Bluf!* ruling.

3.2.2 The Chilling Effect in the UK

Activists have long pointed out that the United Kingdom needs to be concerned about its protection of the right to free speech: For some time these concerns have been centred round the UK's libel law which was perceived to stifle free and frank exchange of ideas. The European Parliament, for example, in May 2012 termed the defamation regime in England and Wales 'the most

---

80. *See*, especially, the judgement in *Lingens v Austria* 8 EHRR 407 (1986) and Valia Filipova, *Standards of Protection of Freedom of Expression and the Margin of Appreciation in the Jurisprudence of the European Court of Human Rights* Cov. L.J. 64 (2012).

81. *Op. cit.*, n 44.

82. Scott Mann (Conservative) at col. 885 and Rob Marris (Labour) at col. 916.

83. *Vereniging Weekblad Bluf! V. the Netherlands* (A/306-A) ECtHR 20 E.H.R.R. 189 (1995).

claimant-friendly in the world'.[84] As such it was argued to have a chilling effect on freedom of expression, in that the mere threat of a libel action could serve as a deterrent to speech. Since such a chilling effect is in reality a form of self-censorship, it is particularly difficult to gauge. Nevertheless, the chilling effect was considered real enough to prompt the wholesale reform of English defamation law, which culminated in the Defamation Act 2013.

It would be ironic if one area of the law is substantially reformed to encourage freedom of speech whilst shortly afterward another legal regime is established that possibly (hopefully) unintentionally reintroduces the chilling effect. The Home Office acknowledges '... the possibility of interception has the ability to discourage freedom of expression and public discourse and therefore interfere with Article 10 rights' but in contrast to its extensive response to privacy concerns raised by campaigners, say little about how Article 10 infringement will be countered.[85]

Conclusion

On the one hand we have legislation that aims to prevent major acts of terrorism partly by curtailing civil rights such as freedom of expression. But how do we judge whether this will work? Can the (so far since the London attacks of 2005 and hopefully continued) absence of major terrorist atrocities in the UK on the scale recently witnessed in Europe and the Middle East be seen as proof of the efficacy of covert and overt surveillance? These operations are by their nature veiled in secrecy—and if they have so far succeeded in preventing crime or terrorist activity, the government is keeping quiet. Anecdotally, it would seem that most of the possible terrorist attacks planned in the UK were prevented through means other than intrusive surveillance: informants, old fashioned boots on the ground police work, and blind luck seem to have been the main bulwarks in this area.[86] On the other hand we have a right, the exer-

---

84. European Parliament Resolution of 10 May 2012 (2013/C 261 E/03), paras C-E.
85. HOME OFFICE, HUMAN RIGHTS MEMORANDUM 2016, *op. cit.*, at 7.
86. For just a few examples of terrorist plots foiled by luck, chance, police work, etc., *see* Marco Giannangelli, *ISIS plot on London, Brighton, Bath and Ipswich FOILED as pilots discuss targets on radio, Express Online* (Jan 25, 2016), available at http://www.express.co.uk/news/uk/637451/RAF-foils-airline-terror-plot-four-British-cities-pop-song-code (last accessed Jun 27, 2016) and Danny Shaw, *Terrorism plot size of 7/7 attacks 'foiled every year'*, *BBC*, (March 21, 2013) available at http://www.bbc.co.uk/news/uk-21878867 (last accessed Jun 27, 2016).

cise of which is difficult if not impossible to gauge. It is difficult to measure whether free speech is or has been chilled—and even more so to predict the likely effect in future. What is certain, and had been convincingly argued before, is that the impact of mass surveillance could potentially affect the exercise of expressive freedoms to such an extent that it may pose a threat to the very idea of democracy itself.[87]

Thomas Jefferson's famous sentiment was that freedom of expression 'cannot be limited without being lost.'[88] Yet experience has shown that absolute freedom of expression either is not workable or comes at (perhaps) too high a price. It already seems as if it is inevitable that in modern life a large degree of indi vidual privacy must be sacrificed on the altar of public security. Will the same fate befall public and private discourse? In effect, what the government seems to be presenting us with is a double bind; the choice between two evils, and its answer with the IP Bill seems to be that less freedom of expression, measured against safety, security and crime, is the lesser of two evils. This is a presumption that cannot be allowed to go unchallenged. The author hopes that at least the same consideration and thought currently being devoted to privacy concerns will be accorded to free speech, before the IP Bill becomes law.

The following sentiment perhaps puts it best:

> "History ... teaches us that ideals (this time the ideal of freedom of speech) that we long for so much have (and could never and nowhere) been realised in full. *Freedom of speech is an ideal, an unattainable mirage* which, as we try to approach it, first loses its contours, then becomes blurry and finally dissipates without a trace in the hot summer air. However, it does not entitle us to quit making increasingly desperate efforts to get closer to it anyway."[89]

---

87. *See* Ronald J. Krotoszynski, Jr., *Reconciling Privacy and Speech in the Era of Big Data: A Comparative Legal Analysis*, 56 WM. & MARY L. REV. 1279, 1287 (2015).

88. Letter to James Currie, 28 January 1786, Library of Congress.

89. KOLTAY, *op. cit.*,96.

Russell L. Weaver[1]
Andras Koltay[2]
Duncan Fairgrieve[3]
Steven I. Friedland[4]

Cybersurveillance: American, Hungarian and British Perspectives

In 2013, the world was shocked when Edward Snowden revealed that the U.S. National Security Agency (NSA) was engaged in a massive secret cybersurveillance and data collection operation.[5] With a budget in excess of $10 billion per year,[6] and 35,000 employees,[7] the NSA was systematically collecting and storing huge amounts of data, including cell phone call records, e-mails, text messages, credit card purchase records and information derived from social media networks.[8] In total, the NSA had intercepted some 182 million communication records.[9] The Snowden revelations stimulated societal debates regarding the extent to which government could or should be involved

---

1. Professor of Law & Distinguished University Scholar, University of Louisville, Louis D. Brandeis School of Law.

2. Associate professor, Pázmány Péter Catholic University, Faculty of Law and Political Sciences (Budapest).

3. Associate Professor of Law, Université Paris Dauphine PSL Research University, & Professor of Law, British Institute International & Comparative Law.

4. Professor of Law & Senior Scholar, Elon University School of Law.

5. *See* Scott Shane, *No Morsel Too Minuscule for All-Consuming NSA: From Spying on Leader of U.N. to tracking Drug Deals, on Ethos of 'Why Not?', The New York Times*, A10 (Nov. 13, 2013); Doug Stanglin; *Snowden Says NSA Can Tap Email Chats, The Courier-Journal*, A3 (Aug. 1, 2013).

6. *See id.*

7. *See id.*

8. *See id.*; *see also* Peter Maass, *How Laura Poitras Helped Snowden Spill His Secrets, The New York Times*, § MM (Aug. 13, 2013); Charlie Savage, *C.I.A. Ties to AT&T's Add Another Side to Spy Debate, International Herald Tribune*, A5 (Nov. 8, 2013).

9. *See* Martha Mendoza, *Reagan's Order Led to NSA's Broader Spying, The Courier-Journal*, A10, c. 1–6 (Nov. 24, 2013).

in surveillance and data collection operations, and ultimately led to limitations on the scope of the NSA's cybersurveillance authority.

The NSA surveillance program raised fundamental questions regarding the relationship between the U.S. government and the U.S. citizenry. Undoubtedly, government has a legitimate interest in investigating and collecting information regarding suspected terrorists. Government also has a legitimate interest in shielding certain types of information (*e.g.*, state secrets or vital information that is potentially damaging to national security or foreign relations) from public scrutiny.[10] However, the question is one of balance. In a democratic society, legitimate questions can be raised regarding the extent to which the government should be involved in such broad-based surveillance, and whether it should be conducting such operations in secret without democratic accountability.

In this short article, we provide American, Hungarian and British perspectives on governmental cybersurveillance and data collection programs. Although everyone now knows about the U.S. cybersurveillance program, many believe that most other societies are conducting similar operations. As a result, in addition to examining the scope of the surveillance programs in each country (to the extent that they are known), we attempt to provide some perspective on societal attitudes towards these programs.

I. U.S. Perspectives

For those who are familiar with the history and founding of the United States, the NSA's cybersurveillance program might have come as a surprise. Although the founders of the U.S. governmental system seemed to embrace democratic principles in the U.S. Declaration of Independence, affirmatively declaring that the power to govern stems from the consent of the governed,[11] and that people have the right to life, liberty and the pursuit of happiness,[12] many were fearful and distrustful of governmental power—even a democratically-elected one.[13] Illustrative were the views of a contemporary writer,

10. *Id.*; *see also United States v. Nixon*, 418 U.S. 683 (1974) (ordering President Nixon to release information, but noting that confidentiality regarding the President's conversations and correspondence is generally privileged, and going on to note that this privilege is "fundamental to the operation of Government and inextricably rooted in the separation of powers under the Constitution.").

11. U.S. Declaration of Independence (July 4, 1776).

12. *Id.*

13. *See* Ralph Ketcham, The Anti-Federalist Papers and the Constitutional Convention Debates: The Clashes and Compromises That Birth to our Govern-

Thomas Paine, who argued that, "Society in every state is a blessing, but government even in its best state is but a necessary evil; in its worst state an intolerable one."[14]

As a result, when the U.S. Constitution was drafted, the Framers went to great lengths to limit and control the scope of federal power. One way they achieved that objective was by embracing the ideas of Baron de Montesquieu, who is credited with articulating the doctrine of separation of powers, and incorporating his ideas into the structure of the Constitution.[15] The Framers believed that separation of powers principles,[16] plus the fact that they had created

---

MENT XV (1986) ("Uncertain that any government over so vast a domain as the United States could be controlled by the people, the anti-federalists saw in the enlarged powers of the central government only the familiar threats to the rights and liberties of the people.").

14. See THOMAS PAINE, COMMON SENSE 3 (1776) (Dover ed. 1997) (In full, the quotation reads as follows: "Society in every state is a blessing, but government even in its best state is but a necessary evil; in its worst state an intolerable one; for when we suffer, or are exposed to the same miseries by a *government*, which we might expect in a country *without government*, our calamity is heightened by reflecting that we furnish the means by which we suffer.").

15. BARON DE MONTESQUIEU, THE SPIRIT OF LAWS 151–152 (Cosimo Edition 2011). He states the theory as follows:

> [There] is no liberty [if] the judiciary power be not separated from the legislative and executive. Were it joined with the legislative, the life and liberty of the subject would be exposed to arbitrary control; for the judge would be then the legislator. Were it joined to the executive power, the judge might behave with violence and oppression.
>
> There would be an end of everything, were the same man or the same body, whether of the nobles or of the people, to exercise those three powers, that of enacting laws, that of executing the public resolutions, and of trying the causes of individuals."

Id.

16. For example, even though Congress was given the power to enact legislation, the Constitution required the President's signature as a prerequisite to enactment (unless Congress overrides the President's veto or the President allows the act to become law without his signature). U.S. CONST., Art. I, Sec. 7 [3]. Likewise, although Congress and the President jointly enact legislation, the judiciary is frequently charged with interpreting that legislation, and sometimes in striking it down. See *Marbury v. Madison*, 5 U.S. (1 Cranch) 137 (1803). Moreover, many powers, such as the foreign affairs power, are shared between the President and Congress. See *United States v. Curtiss Wright Export Corp.*, 299 U.S. 304 (1936). For example, the Senate is charged with ratifying treaties, which the Constitution charges the President with the power to negotiate and make, U.S. CONST., Art. II, Sec. 2 [2], but only the entire Congress can declare war, U.S. CONST., Art. I, Sec. 8 [11], and the President is integrally involved in other foreign affairs issues as well. See *United States v. Curtiss Wright Export Corp.*, 299 U.S. 304 (1936). In addition, the Framers created different terms

a federal government of limited and enumerated powers,[17] would sufficiently protect the people of the United States against governmental overreaching. As a result, they decided to omit as unnecessary a declaration of rights from the text of the Constitution.[18] This decision was met by opposition from those who demanded a formal bill of rights,[19] believing that "without a Bill of Rights guaranteeing individual liberty the new general Government carried with it a potential for tyranny."[20] It was finally agreed that the Constitution should be ratified "as is," in other words without a bill of rights, but that the first Congress would draft one.[21] As a result, the Bill of Rights entered the Constitution as the first ten amendments.[22]

One of the protections demanded as part of the Bill of Rights was a protection against "unreasonable searches and seizures." This demand was ultimately reflected in the Fourth Amendment to the U.S. Constitution[23] which was enacted against a backdrop of colonial abuses.[24] The colonists were particularly riled by the use of "writs of assistance" that allowed British officials to do no more than specify the object of a search,[25] and thereby gain authority to search any place where contraband might be found,[26] without limit as to place or duration.[27] Another reviled practice involved the use of "general warrants" that required colonial officials only to specify an offense, and then left it to the dis-

---

of office for different officials so that a single election could not dramatically shift the course and direction of government. U.S. Const., Art. I, Sec. 2 [1]. See Ralph Ketcham, The Anti-Federalist Papers and the Constitutional Convention Debates: The Clashes and Compromises That Birth to our Government xv (1986) ("Also, mindful of colonial experience and following the arguments of Montesquieu, the idea that the legislative, executive, and judicial powers had to be 'separated,' made to 'check and balance' each other in order to prevent tyranny, gained wide acceptance.").

17. See U.S. Const., Art. I, §8.

18. See *Wallace v. Jaffree*, 472 U.S. 78, 92 (1985) (White, J., dissenting).

19. See *McDonald v. City of Chicago*, 561 U.S. 742 (2010).

20. See *Wallace v. Jaffree*, 472 U.S. 78, 92 (1985) (White, J., dissenting).

21. See *McDonald v. City of Chicago*, 561 U.S. 742 (2010).

22. U.S. Constitution, Amdt. I–X.

23. U.S. Constitution, Amdt. IV.

24. See *Maryland v. Garrison*, 480 U.S. 79, 91 (1987); *Boyd v. United States*, 116 U.S. 616, 625 (1886); see also *United States v. Verdugo-Urquidez*, 494 U.S. 259, 266 (1990).

25. See *Virginia v. Moore*, 553 U.S. 164, 168–169 (2008); *Samson v. California*, 547 U.S. 843, 858 (2006); *Atwater v. City of Lago Vista*, 532 U.S. 318, 339–340 (2001); see also Russell L. Weaver, John M. Burkoff, Catherine Hancock, Jancy Hoeffel, Steven Singer & Steven Friedland, Contemporary Criminal Procedure (2015).

26. See *Atwater v. City of Lago Vista*, 532 U.S. 318, 339–340 (2001).

27. See *Steagald v. United States*, 451 U.S. 204, 221 (1981); *Gilbert v. California*, 388 U.S. 263, 286 (1967).

cretion of executing officials to decide which persons should be arrested and which places should be searched.[28]

Perhaps the most interesting facet of the NSA cybersurveillance program was the fact that it was being conducted in a nation that was founded upon distrust of government, and in which the people had demanded very specific protections against "unreasonable searches and seizures." How could such a country have allowed the government to create a multi-billion dollar cybersurveillance operation that was collecting and storing huge amounts of data? The answer lies, to a large extent, in the U.S. Supreme Court's troubled Fourth Amendment jurisprudence. When the Fourth Amendment was ratified, surveillance technology was comparatively crude and simplistic. The new Americans had been subjected primarily to actual physical searches by British officials of their homes and persons.[29] As a result, the United States Supreme Court's definition of a search tended to track this historical approach by defining the term "search" with reference to people or places.[30] Under these early decisions, the Court held that a search was committed when an individual was physically searched,[31] or the police intruded or trespassed into a "constitutionally protected area."[32] Thus, when the police broke into someone's house and rummaged through its contents, the Court would hold that the police had conducted a Fourth Amendment "search."[33] Likewise, when the police searched the interior of an automobile (once automobiles existed), or they rummaged through an individual's briefcase, the courts would find that the police had engaged in a search within the meaning of the Fourth Amendment.[34]

This historical approach worked fairly well until the invention of electricity, which led to significant advances in surveillance technology. For example, in the early twentieth century, the police began to use a device called the "detectaphone" which allowed them to hear conversations occurring in an adjoining room without actually entering the room.[35] Likewise, about that same time,

---

28. See Moore, supra, 553 U.S. at 168–169; Steagald, supra, 451 U.S. at 220; *Payton v. New York*, 445 U.S. 573 (1980).

29. See *Draper v. United States*, 358 U.S. 307, 318 (1959); see also Garrison, 480 U.S. at 91.

30. See, e.g., *Carroll v. United States*, 267 U.S. 132 (1925); *Hester v. United States*, 265 U.S. 57 (1924).

31. See Draper, 358 U.S. at 307.

32. See, e.g., *Goldman v. United States*, 316 U.S. 129 (1942); *Olmstead v. United States*, 277 U.S. 438 (1928); Ex Parte Jackson, 96 U.S. 727 (1877).

33. See *Silverman v. United States*, 365 U.S. 505, 511–12 (1961).

34. See, e.g., Carroll, 267 U.S. at 132.

35. See *Goldman v. United States*, 316 U.S. 129 (1942).

the police began using wiretaps that allowed them to access conversations occurring over ordinary telephone lines.[36] The police also had access to such devices as "parabolic microphones" which allowed them to hear conversations from three hundred yards away, including experimental sound wave technology whereby police could flood a room with sonic waves making "it possible to overhear everything said in a room without ever entering it or even going near it," and an instrument "which can pick up a conversation through an open office window on the opposite side of a busy street."[37]

For the next half century, the Court struggled to find an approach that could deal with new technologies under its Fourth Amendment jurisprudence. By and large, the Court's efforts were ineffectual.[38] During this period, numerous dissents sounded the alarm regarding the potentially negative implications of the new technologies for personal privacy. For example, in one case, Justice Murphy dissented, arguing that the Framers would have abhorred these new devices because they allowed governmental officials to invade privacy, and intrude on intimate details, in various ways: "by placing on the outer walls of the sanctum a detectaphone that transmits to the outside listener the intimate details of a private conversation, or by new methods of photography that penetrate walls or overcome distances.[39] Justice Brandeis raised similar alarms in his *Olmstead* dissent.[40]

With its decision in *Katz v. United States*,[41] the Court finally formulated a new approach for defining the term "search" under the Fourth Amendment, particularly as that term applied to technology. The Court held that a Fourth Amendment search existed, not only when there was a trespassory invasion into a constitutionally protected area, but also when governmental officials intruded upon an individuals "reasonable expectation of privacy" (REOP).[42]

While *Katz* could have provided individuals with far more protection under the Fourth Amendment, the REOP test has not been expansively construed.

36. See *Olmstead v. United States*, 277 U.S. 438 (1928).

37. Id., at 508–509.

38. See Russell L. Weaver, The James Otis Lecture: The Fourth Amendment, Privacy and Advancing Technology, 80 Miss. L.J. 1131–1227 (2011).

39. Goldman, 316 U.S. at 139–140. He went on to argue that: "Such invasions of privacy, unless they are authorized by a warrant issued in the manner and form prescribed by the Amendment or otherwise conducted under adequate safeguards defined by statute, are at one with the evils which have heretofore been held to be within the Fourth Amendment and equally call for remedial action." Id., at 140.

40. Olmstead, 277 U.S., at 475.

41. 389 U.S. 347 (1967).

42. Id. at 351–352.

Even though there are a few cases in which the Court has construed the decision broadly in a privacy protective way,[43] the Court has generally been reluctant to find that the government has violated an individual's REOP.[44] Indeed, in a number of cases, the Court has restricted the REOP test through various findings and glosses.[45]

Perhaps the most damaging gloss comes from the doctrine which states that an individual does not have a REOP in information that has been voluntarily conveyed to a third party.[46] As a result, if the government seizes the information from that third party, while there may be a search as to the person holding the information, there is no search as to the conveyer. Applied literally, this doctrine would make it difficult for individuals to challenge governmental seizures of their e-mails, text messages, or phone call information, which are routinely sent though various service providers such as Verizon and ATT. That is one of the reasons why the Snowden revelations were regarded as so explosive. Not only was the government sweeping up huge amounts of information, there was arguably no violation of the Fourth Amendment. Moreover, because the Court has restrictively applied standing limitations in actions against the National Security Agency (NSA),[47] it was extremely difficult for individuals to determine the information being collected by the NSA, as well as to challenge that collection.

Even though the Snowden revelations created much public criticism and consternation, especially regarding whether the NSA (or the government generally) should be engaging in widespread secret cyber surveillance data collection operations, the controversy did not lead to radical changes in U.S. law. It did result in Second Circuit Court of Appeals' decision in *ACLU v. Clapper*,[48] which purported to strike down the NSA surveillance and telephone data collection program.

The controversy also led to adoption of the U.S.A. Freedom Act of 2015 in which Congress altered the NSA's surveillance and collection authority. Title I

---

43. See *Kyllo v. United States*, 533 U.S. 27 (2001).

44. See Russell L. Weaver, The James Otis Lecture: The Fourth Amendment, Privacy and Advancing Technology, 80 Miss. L.J. 1131–1227 (2011).

45. Id.

46. See *Smith v. Maryland*, 442 U.S. 735 (1979).

47. See Clapper case.

48. __F.3d ___ (2d Cir. 2015). The three-member panel of the Court held that the government surveillance program collecting bulk telephone metadata resulting from phone calls made by and to Americans exceeded the statutory authority to do so under Section 215 of the PATRIOT Act.

of the Act, FISA Business Records Reforms, adopted a prohibition on bulk collection of tangible things, limiting the collection of call detail (metadata) records.[49] The Title also created two frameworks for the production of records, depending on whether the records are part of an authorized investigation to protect against international terrorism. This Title also included a method for determining the termination of requests. Under Title II of the Act, FISA Pen Register and Trap and Trace Device Reform, there is a similar prohibition of bulk or dragnet collection of some data.[50] The Title generally requires a specific selection term for pen register or trap and trace orders, excluding broad geographic areas or an electronic communication service from serving as a selection term. Title V of the Act, National Security Letter Reform, adopts a limitation on the collection of bulk data pursuant to National Security Letters (NSLs). While part of Title V of the Act limits bulk data collection, another section also limits public disclosure of these letters. This Title allows NSL recipients to challenge requests or nondisclosure requirements.

While the Snowden revelations precipitated hand wringing and some changes in U.S. law in the area of cybersurveillance, other sources of mass surveillance were growing on parallel tracks. Cybersurveillance in the United States has occurred not only through direct government programs, but also through a long history of public-private partnerships.[51] While big technology and telephony companies have been the most important partners of government,[52] consumers and ordinary individuals have facilitated mass surveillance systems as well. This source of data production has occurred primarily through the Internet of Things,[53] which includes wearable technology such as

49. See Section 103 of the Act.

50. See Section 201 of the Act.

51. See David Sanger & Nicole Perlroth, Obama Heads to Security Talks Amid Tensions, N.Y. Times (Feb. 13, 2014), http://www.nytimes.com/ 2015/02/13/business/obama-heads-to-security-talks-amid-tensions.html (last visited June 16, 2015) (noting a "long history of quiet cooperation between Washington and America's top technology companies").

52. According to the cybersecurity coordinator for the Obama Administration, Michael Daniel, "American firms are increasingly concerned about international competitiveness, and that means making a very public show of their efforts to defeat American intelligence gathering by installing newer, harder-to-break encryption systems and demonstrating their distance from the United States government." Id.

53. The Internet of Things refers to devices that generate data and can be operated and adjusted remotely. See, e.g., Kyle Vanhemert, This Brilliant Washing Machine is a Roadmap for the Internet of Things, Wired, (April 7, 2014, 6:30 AM), http://www.wired.com/2014/04/this-brilliant-internet-connected-washer-is-a-roadmap-for-the-internet-of-things/. (describing Cloudwash, a prototype washing machine by Berg Co.).

"smart" watches, "smart" homes that include appliances that are connected to the Internet and each other,[54] and even "smart" buildings that have dual functioning mechanisms to coordinate facility operations. All of these "smart" things, especially cell phones, have created an expanding marketplace for data that is easily accessible, stored, and sorted through software programs.

Private companies have considerable incentive to understand and track the propensities of consumers. The better these commercial companies track customer preferences, the more likely that they can tailor their goods to promote purchases. For example, there is a program called "Radar," produced by the largest owner of outdoor billboards in the country, Clearchannel Outdoors, that tracks persons' cell phones passing by a billboard and then determines whether that person follows up on an advertisement by viewing the subject online or by purchasing the advertised goods.[55]

These programs have been given, sold and sometimes disclosed secretly[56] to the government. One example of a private company's program openly used by the government is 'Beware,' produced by the company, Intrado.[57] The software program calculates a person's "threat" score, using a red light for the most threatening, yellow for somewhat threatening, and green for not threatening. At least one police force in California is now using the software to help officers respond to 911 calls.[58] In short, the government collects its own data, but now

---

54. See, e.g., the Next Thermostat, that determines whether someone is home and automatically adjusts the temperature in the home. The company was recently purchased by Google for 3.2 billion dollars. Josh Ong, Google to Acquire Nest Labs for $3.2 Billion, TNW Blog, Jan. 13, 2014, http://thenextweb.com/google/2014/01/13/google-acquires-nest-3-2-billion/.

55. The company describes Radar as follows: "Using anonymous aggregated data from consumer cellular and mobile devices, RADAR measures consumer's real-world travel patterns and behaviors as they move through their day, analyzing data on direction of travel, billboard viewability, and visits to specific destinations. This movement is then mapped against Clear Channel's displays, allowing advertisers to plan and buy Out-Of-Home to reach specific behavioral audience segments." Merrit Kennedy, "Using Billboards, Company Will Collect Personal Information to Help Advertisers," The Two-Way, NPR (Feb. 29, 2016). http://www.npr.org/sections/thetwo-way/2016/02/29/468598100/using-billboards-company-will-collect-personal-information-to-help-advertisers

56. For example, secret disclosures occur through requests by an agency through a National Security Letter.

57. Chris Weller, "A California Police Department is Using Software to Decide if You Are About to Commit a Crime," Tech Insider (Jan. 12, 2016). Available at: http://www.techinsider.io/intrado-beware-system-tracks-threat-levels-2016-1.

58. Id.

has many other sources open to providing a plethora of information that potentially could be useful.

II. Hungarian Perspectives

Hungary's situation is a bit different than that of the United States. Attempts to protect the people against state attempts to collect intelligence arose in Hungary only after the collapse of the Communist regime in 1990. Although concepts related to the protection of privacy and personal data were already well-established in Western European legal systems by that time, and quickly appeared in Hungarian legislation, Hungarian jurisprudence and the related vigilance of citizens against government came later. With the advent of the Internet, governments obtained enhanced ability to intrude on privacy, and in a less noticeable manner than before. This movement towards greater surveillance increased following the latest emergence of terrorism on the continent. After 2010, significant changes took place in Hungary's laws on the collection of intelligence information, which already were limited by rule of law requirements. This section provides an overview of these amendments, focusing on the Hungarian Constitutional Court and the Strasbourg-based European Court of Human Rights (ECtHR), and their assessment of the amendments in light of existing constitutional and fundamental rights.

A. Hungary's Fundamental Law

Article VI (1) of the Fundamental Law provides comprehensive protections for privacy, including the private and family life of individuals, their homes, their social contacts and reputations. In terms of substance, the general statement of the Constitutional Court describes the essence of privacy, i.e., that the notion of privacy includes that nobody can intrude on or even access it without the individual's consent.[59]

There is a close relationship between the right to privacy afforded by Article VI (1) of the Fundamental Law and the right to human dignity guaranteed by Article II of the Fundamental Law. Article II of the Fundamental Law provides the foundation for the protection of privacy, and prohibits state infringements of that right, since privacy provides the basis for human dignity. Under the Fundamental Law, the protection of privacy is not restricted to the

59. Constitutional Court decision No. 36/2005. (X. 5.).

inner or intimate sphere, which is also protected by Article II of the Fundamental Law, but also extends to the broader sense of privacy (social contacts), and the spatial sphere, where private and family life takes place (the home). In addition, the external aspects of an individual's life also enjoy separate protection (right to reputation).

Article VI of the Fundamental Law provides for the protection of personal data. In its earlier rulings, the Constitutional Court did not view the right to the protection of personal data as a traditional right, but construed it as giving the individual a right of information self-determination. The right to protection of personal data gives everyone the right to decide regarding the disclosure and use of their personal data. The recording and use of personal data is permissible with the data subject's consent; but the data processing path must be traceable and verifiable by everybody who is entitled to information regarding by whom, where and for what purposes their personal data are used. Exceptionally, mandatory disclosure of personal data can be provided for by law as well as by the manner of their use.[60] The right to information self-determination is closely linked to the right to privacy, and includes the right to decide when and subject to what limitations data can be linked to their persons. However, individuals, as social being with social embeddedness, must tolerate the mandatory disclosure of their data to a certain extent, as well as to its use by the state.

The Constitutional Court has specified conditions for restricting the exercise of the right to information self-determination as contrasted with the usual test applied when government restricts fundamental rights (necessity-proportionality). For example, the court has imposed a "purpose" limitation, as a condition precedent, and has also imposed the most important guarantee for the exercise of the right to informational self-determination. Effectively, these rules mean that personal data can only be collected for precisely specified and lawful purposes. Data processing must comply with the notified purpose as recorded in a public register, in every phase of the processing. It follows from the purpose limitation that any collection and storage of data in the absence of a specified purpose, for a future use not specified in advance, is unconstitutional.[61]

The Constitutional Court has not previously ruled regarding the permissibility of collecting intelligence information under the Act on National Security Services,[62] when it is carried out for other than law enforcement pur-

60. Constitutional Court decision No. 15/1991. (IV 13.).
61. Constitutional Court decision No. 15/1991. (IV. 13.).
62. Act CXXV of 1995 on the National Security Services.

poses. Nevertheless, in Constitutional Court decision No. 2/2007. (I. 24.), the court outlined general criteria governing the means and methods of collecting intelligence information that are acceptable under the democratic rule of law.

> The use of collecting information using intelligence and acquisition of data using intelligence methods as criminal law instruments under the democratic rule of law is based on the circumstance that traditional instruments proved to be inadequate to act successfully against certain crimes seriously violating or endangering the order of society. In order to protect society, methods and instruments are needed that can make up for any possible strategic disadvantage that law enforcement bodies can have against crime. The restriction of fundamental rights under review by the methods applied in intelligence procedures is not an unnecessary instrument in constitutional terms. However, the protection of the rule of law and fundamental rights require that the procedure for using these instruments is regulated by the law in detail and in a differentiated manner. Since the use of these intelligence instruments means a grave intrusion into the privacy of individuals, their application can take place only exceptionally, as a temporary and ultimate solution.[63]

The broad-ranging rules governing intelligence instruments are set forth in the individual acts governing the bodies authorized to use them, including the Police Act,[64] the Act on the National Security Services, the Act on the Criminal Procedure, the Act on the Public Prosecutor's Office and the Act on the National Tax and Customs Authority.

B. General Rules on the Collection of Information Using Intelligence

The legislation differentiates between the *collection of intelligence information* and the *acquisition of data using intelligence method*; however, the legislation does not contain any definitions. Regarding the basis for regulating these two methods of collecting intelligence information, distinctions are made between collecting information using intelligence obtained before initiation of the investigation, and the acquisition of data using intelligence methods developed after the initiation of an investigation but before charges are laid.

63. Constitutional Court decision No. 2/2007. (I. 24.), 65, 100.
64. Act XXXIV of 1994 on the Police.

The regulation provides for two different processes for collecting intelligence information: one for *law enforcement purposes* and the other for *purposes other than law enforcement*. Collection of intelligence for purposes other than law enforcement may be subject to external authorization[65] or it might not be.[66] When authorization is required by law, the authorization must come from a judge or the Minister of Justice.

The law mandates a split external authorization system. If the government seeks to detect a specific crime, the collection of intelligence information must be authorized by a judge appointed by the Chairman of the Metropolitan Court of Budapest. Other activities, involving the general collection of information, must be authorized by the Minister of Justice.

Collection of intelligence information is allowed if the data is required to perform tasks mandated by law that cannot be acquired in other ways. However, it is possible to obtain exceptional authorization under Article 59 of Act on the National Security Services. If the delay caused by the authorization procedure would deprive the Security Services of the chance to detect crime, or uncover evidence in a specific case, the interests in the effective operation of the National Security Service, the General Director of the National Security Service can authorize the collection of intelligence information under Article 56, parallel with the submission of a proposal for the authorization, pending the decision of the Minister of Justice or the judge.

Article 56 of the Act on the National Security Services lists the intelligence instruments and methods that can be deployed subject to external authorization:

a) search of a private dwelling, recording any detection by way of technical devices;

b) monitoring and recording of events in a private dwelling using technical devices;

c) opening a postal consignment, or opening and checking a sealed consignment that can be linked to an identified person, and recording its content using technical devices;

d) becoming aware of the content of a communication forwarded by electronic communication services, and recording the detected content using technical devices;

e) becoming aware, recording and use of data forwarded via or stored on IT devices or systems.

65. Act CXXV of 1995 on the National Security Services, Articles 54, 55.
66. Ibid., Articles 56 to 60.

Under the Act on National Security Services, a proposal for authorization to collect intelligence information can be submitted by the Director General of the Information Office, the Constitution Protection Office, the Military National Security Service, and, for specified tasks, the National Security Special Service.[67] The Act states that the judge and the Minister responsible for judicial matters shall make a decision within 72 hours following the submission of the proposal, and shall either uphold the proposal or reject it if unfounded.[68] No appeal can be lodged against the authorizing decision so that the person proposing the authorization has no remedy against an adverse decision. Indeed, the affected person is not entitled to access the decision, since the authorizing body cannot inform the person concerned regarding its procedure or even the fact that the collection of intelligence information is taking place.

The authorizing body may grant authorization to collect intelligence information for up to 90 days per occasion, a deadline that can be extended in justified cases based on a new proposal for a further 90 days, for an unlimited number of occasions.[69] The National Security Committee of the Parliament exercises control over the authorization procedure performed by the Minister of Justice.[70]

C. The new Counter Terrorism Body

On 1 September 2010, the Government established the Counter Terrorism Centre (*Terrorelhárítási Központ*, TEK). TEK has nationwide jurisdiction and operates under the control of the Minister responsible for policing (Minister for Internal Affairs). Based on the nature of its activities, TEK is a public authority and, according to its charter, is an independent, autonomous budgetary body. The regulation defines the fight against terrorism as the task of the entire police force, into which TEK is integrated.

The Police Act creates the legal basis for the TEK's collection of intelligence information, and provides that the counter-terrorism body can collect intelligence,[71] and transforms the authorization framework for the collection of intelligence. The counter-terrorism body can, in the performance of its tasks (which involve the prevention of terrorist acts, supplemented by the authority to collect information related to Hungarian citizens who are in trouble

---

67. Ibid., Article 57 (1)
68. Ibid., Article 58 (3)
69. Ibid., Article 58 (4)
70. Ibid., Article 14 (4)
71. Police Act, Article 7/E (2).

abroad), and can collect information using intelligence methods. The counter-terrorism body, in performance of its tasks relating to the prevention of terrorism, can collect information applying the Act on National Security Services *mutatis mutandis*. During the performance of its tasks, the TEK is entitled to request and process data in line with the Act on National Security Services. Collection of information using intelligence methods can be authorized by the Minister of Justice.

D. Decision of the Constitutional Court

In Constitutional Court Decision No. 323/2013. (VI. 22.), the applicants challenged the collection of intelligence information by the counter terrorism body for purposes other than law enforcement. They claimed that the challenged provision violated the Fundamental Law because it allows the counter-terrorism bodies to collect intelligence information without ensuring the enforcement of fundamental rights that are absent from the Act on National Security Services. The applicants objected that the authorization by the Minister responsible for judicial matters failed to provide appropriate guarantees, in particular that the reasons for the request for authorization were not set forth in legal terms.

The Constitutional Court therefore was asked to examine, in the framework of the application, whether the authorization for the counter-terrorism body to collect intelligence information by the Minister responsible for judicial matters violated the fundamental right to privacy and the right of informational self-determination.

The Constitutional Court first examined the constitutionality of the authorization to collect intelligence information by the Minister responsible for judicial matters. The first phase is an order of intervention. In view of the fact that the Minister responsible for judicial matters approves, by authorizing the instruments and methods to be used in the collection of intelligence information, a state intervention that seriously violates fundamental rights, the authorization must meet several requirements: its procedure must be regulated by law; it must comply with the clarity of the norms requirement; and it must contain external control mechanisms.

The Court held that the right to the protection of privacy and the right of informational self-determination are not unrestricted fundamental rights. Intrusion on privacy and the use of data can be justified by both law enforcement and national security objectives. In the meanwhile, the individual is required to tolerate the restriction of fundamental rights to the extent the restriction has a legal constitutional basis.

Despite being a policing body, the counter-terrorism body can collect intelligence not only for law enforcement purposes, but also for national security purposes. The challenged rule in the Police Act grants authorization to the counter-terrorism body to collect information using intelligence in the framework of its set tasks, under the Act on National Security Services. The obligation to obtain authorization from the Minister responsible for judicial matters is related to the enforcement of a national security interest. The legal definition of the term "national security interest" expressly refers to the acquisition of information on foreign states or of foreign origin, which is required for Government decisions, and the detection and prevention of terrorist acts.[72]

In the opinion of the Constitutional Court, national security tasks include a much wider range of activities than just law enforcement tasks; they do not primarily examine the criminal law relevance of events and do not necessarily generate consequences in criminal procedure. The country has a legitimate interest in detecting and preventing individuals from committing certain acts even if the individuals may not have committed specific crimes. Hence, the task of protecting national security cannot be compared with collecting intelligence for law enforcement purposes as authorized by a judge. Prevention of, and protection against, national security risks require political decisions, and as such, fall within the competence of the Executive. In the Court's view, the Act on National Security Services authorizes the Minister responsible for judicial matters to authorize the collection of general intelligence information collection.

When granting authorization for national security purposes, the Minister responsible for judicial matters must weigh the national security interest against any potential violation of fundamental rights. The authorizing body must, in addition to considering the protection of the country's security interests and taking policy aspects (both internal and external), balance the interests in national security and fundamental rights. When doing so, it departs from the rule that the counter terrorism body can use intelligence methods for national security purposes as an ultimate detection instrument. It can also use special instruments and methods of collecting intelligence information only if the data required to perform the tasks cannot be otherwise acquired, i.e. by using traditional investigative measures. The above-referenced red provision of the Act on National Security Services provides the legal guarantee by setting forth those crimes in law for which the collection of intelligence information is allowed for law enforcement purposes based on the existence of a suspected crime.

72. Act CXXV of 1995 on the National Security Services, Article 74, Subsections (a) (ac) and (ae)

External control is an essential requirement for ordering and implementing the collection of intelligence information. The Parliament's National Security Committee exercises control over the counter-terrorism body's activities, performed through application of the rules set forth in the Act on National Security Services. When the Committee suspects that these activities have been carried out unlawfully or improperly, it can request an inquiry from the Minister who must report the results of the inquiry to the Committee. If an unlawful operation is detected, it can carry out fact finding investigations.

Under Act CXI of 2011 on the Commissioner for Fundamental Rights, the authority for policing bodies, including the counter-terrorism body, are under the competence of the Ombudsman.[73] Nothing may stand in the way of an Ombudsman inquiry. There is only one limitation set forth in the Act: its report on the examination of bodies that are authorized to use intelligence instruments and methods cannot contain data that reveals the information collected by the body in a specific case.[74]

On the basis of the above, the Constitutional Court has held that the Act on National Security Services provides control over the authorization procedures performed by the Minister responsible for judicial matters by bodies independent from the Executive. In view of the above, the Constitutional Court dismissed the motion to establish the violation of the Fundamental Law. The authorization by the Minister regarding the counter-terrorism body's specific national security tasks formed an integral part of the regulatory concept as represented in the Act on National Security Services. This concept cannot be challenged under constitutional law.

E. Ruling by the ECtHR

The issue of competence rules was brought before the ECtHR by two constitutional lawyers. In their submission, they claimed that there is a chance of intelligence information being collected against them, resulting in an unjustified and disproportionate restriction on their right to privacy. The ECtHR admitted this motion, concluding that the regulation at stake could potentially affect all users of communication systems (potential concern), and that the legal regulations failed to guarantee the rights of individuals to challenge these measures when they suspect that they are under surveillance. In view of these two aspects, the ECtHR concluded that the applicants could rightfully refer to

73. Act CXI of 2011, Article 18 81 (1) (f)

74. Ibid., Article 28 (3).

the violation of their rights guaranteed in the European Convention of Human Rights.

The ECtHR found that guarantees related to the collection of information contained in the Police Act were insufficient.[75] In the Court's view, the law provides for the surveillance of anybody, even a large population group, since the public authority is not required in the authorization to prove a connection between a person who is a target of surveillance and a potential terror threat or national security risk. On the other hand, the public authority is not required to provide a reasonable justification for the surveillance. Furthermore, surveillance for 90 days can be extended by a further 90 days. It is unclear whether this extension can take place only once or more than once.

The most serious concern involves the lack of judicial control over the authorization procedure. The judges in Strasbourg concluded that authorization by a minister, who belongs to the Executive, and therefore in the chain of political power, is not a sufficient guarantee against the possibility of abuse. External judicial control of surveillance is regarded as the most secure guarantee of independence, impartiality and fair procedure.

The ECtHR concluded that the Minister's obligation to report to the Parliament's National Security Committee, and the limited investigative competences of the Ombudsman, cannot be regarded as sufficient guarantees. The Court found that the complaint against the Act on National Security Services was justified since the subject of surveillance are not informed that they are under surveillance.

In view of the above, and given the current level of technological advancement, and the fact that the Government can accumulate vast amounts of information on individuals other than those who are the targets of monitoring, the ECtHR found a violation of Article 8 of the Convention.

F. Conclusions Regarding Hungary

The regulation, and the issues arising from it, relating to the constitutional guarantees relating to surveillance, illustrate the current state of the Hungarian legal system. To date, the legislation has not been amended following the January 2016 ruling of the Strasbourg Court, but amendment will ultimately be necessary. There is a tension between the state's interest in quick and unbiased decision making and observance of rule of law guarantees securing the

75. *Szabó and Vissy v. Hungary*, app. no. 37138/14, judgment of 12 January 2016.

right to privacy. States are reluctant to resolve this tension by restricting the margin of error (room for manoeuvre) of the Government. Luckily, so far, Hungary has only been indirectly affected by the fight against terror which is taking place at the European level, and these relatively peaceful times allow rule of law guarantees to mature and establish themselves. We hope that we will never find out how the government will respond or limit guarantees if disaster strikes.

III. The United Kingdom

The Snowden revelations had a particular impact in the United Kingdom with the general public finally understanding and appreciating the extent of governmental surveillance in the UK. Specific concerns arose about the way in which the governmental communications agency, GCHQ, was intercepting the communications of the general public in a routine and large-scale manner. A very valuable analysis of this and related issues is found in the influential report produced by David Anderson QC, the Independent Reviewer of Terrorism Legislation, entitled *A Question of Trust: Report of the Investigatory Powers Review*, and published in June 2015. The purpose of this report was to inform the public and political debate on the effectiveness of existing legislation relating to investigatory powers and to set out proposals for reform.

A. Context—The Legal Position in the United Kingdom

Constitutional and Legal Background in Summary. The position of the UK is complicated by the lack of a single constitutional document, and this has thus had an impact on the legal provisions concerning the law on investigatory powers. Common law constraints on executive action regarding the collection of data have foundered on the complexity of the pre-existing framework. Focus was initially placed on a series of 18th Century cases on general warrants,[76] as a potential means for providing a legal framework for the collection of data, but claimants failed to establish a right to protection for private communications. As has been recognised in one influential report, "the surprising outcome is that the common law, shorn of the influence of the ECHR, barely recognises the right to privacy or private communications."[77]

76. e.g., Entick v Carrington 95 ER 807.

77. A Question of Trust: Report of the Investigatory Powers Review (Independent Reviewer of Terrorism Legislation, June 2015) para 5.11.

A word must thus be said of the Convention rights, with particular relevance here of Articles 6 (right to a fair trial), 8 (right to respect for private and family life), and 10 (freedom of expression). Unsurprisingly, the ECtHR has held that the collections of communications data and the interception of content of communications interfere with Article 8.[78] The bulk collection of data has been examined by the ECtHR on fewer occasions, but the court has again opined that: "the case law of the ECtHR suggests that bulk data collection and analysis, in the absence of suspicion, is not in itself a disproportionate interference with the right to respect for private life. However, bulk collection will be assessed against a higher standard than individual interferences with the right to privacy. The justification for that interference, and the safeguards in place to prevent abuse, will need to be more compelling if the requirements of Article 8(2) are to be satisfied."[79] Under EU law, both the Charter of Fundamental Rights[80] and data protection law[81] are relevant to the law on investigatory powers.

Specific Statutory framework for the interception of telecommunications or communications data.[82] In the United Kingdom, the statutory provisions relating to investigatory powers are complex and heterogeneous. The statutory authority for the interception of telecommunications or communications data is provided by the Regulation of Investigatory Powers Act 2000 ("RIPA"). Under RIPA, there are various mechanisms for authorizing the interception and acquisition of communications data. In typical common law fashion, the Secretary of State has published Guidance for the use of these powers, including the Interception of Communications Code of Practice,[83] the Acquisition and Disclosure of Communications Data Code of Practice,[84] and the Retention of Communications Data Code of Practice.[85]

---

78. E.g., Malone v United Kingdom (1984) 7 EHRR 14.

79. A Question of Trust: Report of the Investigatory Powers Review (Independent Reviewer of Terrorism Legislation, June 2015) para 5.34.

80. See Articles 7 and 8 of the EU Charter.

81. See, e.g., Data Protection Directive 95/46 EC.

82. See also the excellent paper of Mariette Jones, "Double-Lock or Double-Bind? The Investigatory Powers Bill and Freedom of Expression in the United Kingdom."

83. Home Office, January 2016. This Code provides guidance on procedures to be followed before the interception of communications can take place under RIPA.

84. Home Office, March 2015. This Code provides guidance on procedures to be followed when acquisition of communications data takes place under RIPA.

85. Home Office, March 2015. This Code provides guidance on procedures to be followed when acquisition of communications data is retained under RIPA.

Although it is in principle illegal to intercept communications, or to obtain information about the use made of a telecommunications service (without the consent of the user),[86] certain public authorities have received statutory authorisation to collect and analyse communications. The current framework concerning investigatory powers has developed in a piecemeal fashion. This will be set out in brief summary here.

The primary statutory framework for the interception of telecommunications is RIPA which provides for a variety of different mechanisms for the authorisation of interception and acquisition of communications data. The primary means by which an interception may be authorised under RIPA is via a warrant which must be signed by a Secretary of State. A variety of organisations may apply for such a warrant, including MI5, MI6, and GCHQ as well as various police services, HMRC and the MoD. In order to authorise an interception, the Secretary of State must believe that the warrant is necessary on the grounds of national security, the prevention or detection of serious crime, or for safeguarding the economic well-being of the UK.[87] The Secretary of State must also believe that the interception is necessary and proportionate to the objective sought, requirements drawn directly from the Article 8 ECHR requirements referred to above. Two different types of warrants can be granted under RIPA, a targeted warrant referenced to "one person as the interception subject" or "a single set of premises",[88] and bulk warrants, often referred to as "external" warrants, which authorise interception of communications where one or both of the senders or recipients of a communication are located outside the British Islands. As has been observed, "such Section 8(4) warrants may be used to authorise the interception of all communications transmitted on a specified route or cable or carried by a particular service provider."[89] Such bulk or Section 8(4) warrants are issued by the Foreign Secretary to GCHQ and thus provide the legal basis for GCHQ's bulk interception capacity. Very large volumes of communications can be intercepted and examined under a Section 8(4) warrant.[90]

86. See Sections 1(1) and 1(2) Regulation of Investigatory Powers Act 2000.

87. See Section 5(3) RIPA.

88. See Section 8(1). These warrants may authorize the interception of communications between two people in the British Islands, the communications of known individuals who are communicating outside the British Islands or between two persons overseas.

89. A Question of Trust: Report of the Investigatory Powers Review (Independent Reviewer of Terrorism Legislation, June 2015) para 6.45.

90. See generally A Question of Trust: Report of the Investigatory Powers Review (Independent Reviewer of Terrorism Legislation, June 2015) para 6.49.

Over and above the statutory framework of RIPA, there are other parallel statutes which permit the interception and acquisition of communications data, in particular the Wireless Telegraphy Act 2006 (WTA 2006) which grants the Secretary of State and the Commissioners of Revenue and Customs a very broad power to authorise the interception of wireless and other communications.[91] Interception must be necessary for a series of statutory purposes, including prevention of crime and disorder.[92] Various concerns were raised by David Anderson QC, Independent Reviewer of Terrorism Legislation, as regards these non-RIPA investigatory powers, in particular that it seemed that certain public authorities exercised those powers without any published Code of Practice in place, and that there was in certain cases the possibility of concurrent use of the powers under RIPA and non-RIPA provisions.[93]

There are various safeguards and oversight procedures built into the mechanisms. In terms of oversight, reference must be made to the Interception of Communications Commissioner (IOCC) and the Investigatory Powers Tribunal.

The Interception of Communications Commissioner is responsible for reviewing the interception of communications and the acquisition and disclosure of communications data by intelligence agencies, police forces and other public authorities.[94] The IOCC thus holds the public authorities that exercise RIPA powers to account and seeks to improve compliance through its oversight and scrutiny. The Commissioner is a serving or retired judge, and the current holder of the office is Sir Stanley Burnton. The Commissioner reports to the Prime Minister on a half-yearly basis with respect to the carrying out of the Interception of Communications Commissioner's functions.

The Investigatory Powers Tribunal was set up under RIPA to investigate and determine complaints of unlawful use of interception of communications and gathering of communications data, as well as complaints under Section 7 of the HRA in respect of intelligence or law enforcement agencies. After a slow start, the Investigatory Powers Tribunal has gradually become an important aspect of oversight of investigatory powers.[95]

---

91. Note also the powers contained in the Telecommunications Act 1984, section 94.

92. The authority to intercept may be granted to any persons that the designated authority considers appropriate. The relationship between WTA 2006 and RIPA is unclear, and the Independent Reviewer of Terrorism Legislation concludes that in principle both RIPA and WTA might be used to intercept the same communications: ibid, para 6.12.

93. Ibid., para 6.20.

94. For further details, see: http://www.iocco-uk.info/

95. See discussion in A Question of Trust: Report of the Investigatory Powers Review (Independent Reviewer of Terrorism Legislation, June 2015) para 6.105—6.111.

C. Comparative Law Position

When undertaking his review of the law relating to investigatory powers, as referred to above, the Independent Reviewer of Terrorism Legislation made some comparative law reflections on interception, access to communications data, and communications data retention. An initial comparison was made with the legal position in Australia, Canada, New Zealand, and the USA which form part of the Five Eyes partnership. Space and time prevent a detailed analysis of that here,[96] but one significant comparative conclusion was the prominence of judicial authorisation in those other jurisdictions: "[i]n contrast to the UK position, criminal law enforcement bodies in the United States, Canada, Australia and New Zealand must all obtain judicial authorisation before they carry out interception."[97] It is thus concluded that "the UK is unique in the Five Eyes in making no use of judges for the prior authorisation of interception warrants. But there is no single standard applied by the other members."[98] In Continental Europe, the picture is mixed but judicial authorisation is not universal.[99]

D. Reforms Underway

Highly influenced by the report produced by David Anderson QC, the Independent Reviewer of Terrorism Legislation in June 2015, the Government announced the enactment of a new piece of legislation, The Investigatory Powers Bill. This legislation is currently going through the parliamentary process and is aimed at providing a new framework for the use of investigatory powers by the executive. The proposed legislation is covered in detail in the excellent paper by Mariette Jones, to which readers are referred[100] and only a brief word will be said here.

The draft legislation is detailed and complex, including the main provisions as well as the schedules and six draft Codes of Practice. The Bill illustrates an attempt by the government to put investigatory powers on a clearer statutory footing as well as to reinforce the relevant safeguards, and oversight.

---

96. See generally A Question of Trust: Report of the Investigatory Powers Review (Independent Reviewer of Terrorism Legislation, June 2015) paras 8.38—8.64.

97. Ibid, para 8.44.

98. Ibid, para 8.47.

99. Ibid, para 8.48.

100. Mariette Jones, "Double-Lock or Double-Bind? The Investigatory Powers Bill and Freedom of Expression in the United Kingdom."

The center-piece of the legislation is the 'double-lock' process, and a word will be said about that here. The 'double-lock' process in essence means that warrants will be issued by the Secretary of State but will not come into force until approved by a Judicial Commissioner (former or serving judges), who will review the according to the principles applicable on judicial review. We will not examine in detail the critique of this new approach here, but it is worth repeating the concerns of the Bingham Centre as follows:[101]

> The problem with the 'double-lock' as proposed is that it does not provide a suitable safeguard on the exercise of power by the Secretary of State because the balance of power to authorise weighs too heavily in favour of the executive. As well as being a Judicial Commissioner model where appointment is executive-driven (rather than authorisation by a judge *per se* who has judicial independence in the accepted sense), the standard of review is that of judicial review, and the judge must authorise in the absence of finding irrationality (in the Wednesbury unreasonable sense), albeit with the caveat that necessity and proportionality will be considered in the equation the more that an authorisation would result in an infringement of rights. Moreover, it is not necessary that the executive hold this degree of power. Authorisation should be by Judicial Commissioners, on the application of the Secretary of State.

Conclusion

As the foregoing discussion reveals, the electronic era has fostered widespread governmental surveillance of the citizenry in most nations. In the U.S., the NSA operates a massive operation that historically has selected huge amounts of information, including information relating to emails, text messages and phone calls. While the NSA claims to be focused on foreigners, the NSA's operations undoubtedly sweep in U.S. citizens at times. Moreover, there are insufficient protections for individual privacy. The program is generally conducted in secrecy, and U.S. courts have placed few restrictions on governmental authority.

In Hungary, the government has passed several pieces of legislation that seek to balance the individual interest in privacy against the governmental in-

101. Written evidence submitted by the Bingham Centre for the Rule of Law to Public Bill Committee (IPB 32), para 15. The report is available as follows: http://www.publications.parliament.uk/pa/cm201516/cmpublic/investigatorypowers/Memo/IPB32.htm

terest in fighting crime and terrorism. Although those laws provide for specific procedures and limitations designed to ensure individual privacy, it is not clear that the Hungarian balance favors privacy. More experience with the new laws will be required to determine their meaning.

In the UK, the Snowden revelations have also made the British public more aware of governmental cybersurveillance, and the fact that GCHQ was intercepting communications in a routine and large-scale manner. Of course, the situation in the UK is complicated by the absence of a single constitutional document, and common law constraints on executive action regarding the collection of data have not provided an effective check on governmental author ity. However, the ECtHR establishes that the collection of communications data and the interception of the content of communications interferes with Article 8. Nevertheless, certain public authorities have received statutory authorisation to collect and analyze communications. However, the current framework for governing the law concerning investigatory powers has developed in a piecemeal fashion. In order to authorize an interception, the Secretary of State must believe that the warrant is necessary on the grounds of national security, the prevention or detection of serious crime, or for safeguarding the economic well-being of the UK. The Secretary of State must also believe that the interception is necessary and proportionate to the objective sought, requirements which draw directly on the Article 8 ECHR requirements. There are also other parallel statutes which allow for the interception and the acquisition of communications data, in particular the Wireless Telegraphy Act 2006 (WTA 2006) which grants the Secretary of State and the Commissioners of Revenue and Customs a very broad power to authorize the interception of wireless and other communications. Interception must be necessary for a series of statutory purposes, including the prevention of crime and disorder. However, concerns were expressed that certain public authorities exercised those powers without any published Code of Practice in place even though there are certain safeguards and oversight procedures built into the mechanisms. In addition, the Investigatory Powers Tribunal was set up under RIPA to investigate and determine complaints of unlawful use of interception of communications and gathering of communications data, as well as complaints under Section 7 of the HRA in respect of intelligence or law enforcement agencies. In addition, there is a law currently going through the parliamentary process which is designed to provide a new framework for the use of executive investigatory powers. The draft legislation is detailed and complex, and illustrates an attempt by the government to put investigatory powers on a clearer statutory footing as well as to reinforce the relevant safeguards, and oversight.

The centerpiece of the legislation is the 'double-lock' process which means that warrants are issued by the Secretary of State, but do not come into force until approved by a Judicial Commissioner (former or serving judges), who will review the according to the principles applicable on judicial review. However, concerns have been expressed regarding the effectiveness of the "double lock" process.

Cristina Pauner Chulvi[1]

Surveillance Capabilities of Drone Technology and Law Enforcement Uses: Implications on Data Protection Within the European Framework[2]

1. Introduction

Drones have become a hot topic of public discussion, primarily because of their controversial use in military operations to perpetrate so-called "targeted killings,"[3] as well as because of their increasing use in domestic markets for purposes ranging from law enforcement to personal entertainment.

Drones, also known as unmanned aerial vehicles (UAV) or remotely piloted aircraft systems (RPAS), constitute a promising technology with potential benefits for European industries and citizens, but they are also of concern because of their potential impact on privacy and data protection. These devices can be equipped with a variety of technologies that offer a wide range of civil applications for state, professional and commercial or recreational purposes. Thanks to their versatility, affordability and multiple capabilities, the market

---

1. Associated Professor of Constitutional Law, Universitat Jaume I. Castellón

2. This paper was elaborated within the framework of CRISP Project funded by the European Commission (Grant num. 607941) and the Research Project on "The Impact of the New General Data Protection Regulation: National and Comparative Analysis", supported by the Spanish Ministry of Economy and Competitiveness (Ref. DER2015-65635-R).

3. On this issue, see SÁNCHEZ DE LA CRUZ, C., "U.S. drone strikes in the FATA region of Pakistan: legality and human impact", *Cuaderno Electrónico de Estudios Jurídicos*, n. 4, 2015, pp. 103–150; McNEAL, G. S., "Targeted killings and accountability", *The Georgetown Law Journal*, vol. 102, 2014, pp. 681–794 and BACHMANN, S. D., "Targeted Killings: Contemporary Challenges, Risks and Opportunities", *Journal of Conflict & Security Law*, n. 2, 2013, pp. 259–288.

of drones is expected to have a strong impact on the global economy, providing a source of economic growth and industrial competitiveness. The most optimistic forecasts suggest that the potential market for drones is more than 127.000 million dollars worldwide (112.331 million euros).[4]

Initially, the paramount objective of the world aviation authorities was that drone safety should be equivalent to that for regular, manned aviation.[5] In recent years, however, there is a perceptible normative movement in Europe that is focused on defending the fundamental rights of citizens, notably, protection of personal data and privacy.[6] The objective is to eliminate gaps found in national regulations that limit the threat of unmanned aircraft to public safety and the privacy of citizens.[7]

There are several European countries that have already passed regulations governing civilian drone operations. According to Eurocontrol,[8] such regulations exist in Germany, Austria, Belgium, Croatia, Denmark, Finland, France, Ireland, Italy, The Netherlands, United Kingdom, Czech Republic, Sweden and Switzerland. Spain has enacted a temporary regulation that took effect in July 2014. The Spanish executive has prepared new legislation that extends the possibilities for use of these vehicles, but the legislation is still pending approval.

One of the main civilian uses for drones is for surveillance. The characteristics of flexibility, mobility, discretion, cost-efficiency and ever more sophisticated payloads make drones unique tools for covert and effective observation

---

4. PwC: "World Drone Market Seen Nearing $127B in 2020", 11 May 2016.

5. The rules covering drones are currently set at global level by the International Civil Aviation Organisation (ICAO), the UN body dealing with civil aviation. Within the EU, the use of drones less than 150 kilograms and the use of all types of drones for *security* or military purposes are regulated by the Member States. The European Aviation Safety Agency (EASA) shall lay down the regulation of the use of larger drones with a mass exceeding 150 kilograms for commercial purposes.

6. The same trend to privacy can be observed in the United States. On 22 May 2015, the U.S. Department of Justice announced agency-wide guidelines that set standards for the domestic use of drones while still respecting the civil rights of American citizens.

7. First European discussions on drones began in 2012 with the adoption of the Commission Staff Working Document *Towards a European Strategy for the development of Civil Applications of Remotely Piloted Aircraft Systems (RPAS)*, but the key document presenting the European strategy on the future regulation on drones is the *Communication A new era for aviation: Opening the aviation market to the civil use of remotely piloted aircraft systems in a safe and sustainable manner* adopted by the European Commission in 2014.

8. Eurocontrol, https://easa.europa.eu/unmanned-aircraft-systems-uas-and-remotely-piloted-aircraft-systems-rpas.

and data gathering. Indeed, many law enforcement agencies in European countries are already deploying drones to perform their security tasks,[9] but drone fever has expanded to other sectors and private companies, as well as individuals and small professional entities such as detective agencies or insurance companies are using drones for security purposes resulting in what has been tagged as the "privatization of surveillance."[10]

Because of this growth, surveillance drones have been the subject of a bitter debate between stakeholders and regulators, giving rise to new legislation designed to protect citizens' privacy. However, security interests are often suggested as a legitimate reason for restraining or even infringing human rights, and include such concepts as public safety, prevention of crime and national defence. In this sense, the European Council has even affirmed that "security is in itself a basic human right"[11] and that the balance between these rights must be assured. In addition, the European Convention of Human Rights provides the possibility for limiting rights under strict conditions (Article 8.2 ECHR).

The security exception is also visible within the new package on data protection rules in the EU, the General Data Protection Regulation (GDPR),[12] which will replace the 1995 Directive which is already obsolete due to the technological and digital revolution, and the Police and Criminal Justice Data Protection Directive,[13] which updates the legislative framework in the EU for these sectors and replaces Council Framework Decision 2008/977/HAA.[14]

---

9. A 2014 Statewatch report estimates that the European Commission had budgeted 315 million euros for the deployment of drones used mainly for surveillance missions by European law enforcement authorities.

10. EPIC Org., "Domestic Unmanned Aerial Vehicles (UAVs) and Drones 2013".

11. European Council, *Internal Security Strategy for the EU: Towards an Internal Security Model*, March 2010, p. 9.

12. Regulation (EU) 2016/679 of the European Parliament and of the Council of 27 April 2016 on the protection of natural persons with regard to the processing of personal data and on the free movement of such data, and repealing Directive 95/46/EC (General Data Protection Regulation).

13. Directive (EU) 2016/680 on the protection of natural persons with regard to the processing of personal data by competent authorities for the purposes of the prevention, investigation, detection or prosecution of criminal offences or the execution of criminal penalties, and on the free movement of such data, and repealing Council Framework Decision 2008/977/JHA (Police and Criminal Justice Data Protection Directive). The Regulation and the Directive entered into force on May 2016 but shall apply from May 2018.

14. We must also mention the European Commission *Proposal for a European Border and Coast Guard Authority*, 15 December 2015, that brings together a reinforced and renamed Frontex–the European Border and Coast Guard Agency–and the Member States' border guard authorities under the umbrella of a European Border and Coast Guard. Al-

In this paper, we focus on the privacy and data protection implications of law enforcement use of surveillance drones. For us, the main concern in the surveillance context is the broad definition given to the concept of security as a legitimate basis for restricting privacy and data protection provisions. The definitional problem is hampered by the appearance of new intrusive security technologies which do not receive adequate discussion in the national—and very heterogeneous—regulations of the Member States. Section 2 introduces the definition of drone, its characteristics and the main application of drones in civil areas. Section 3 involves an exploratory study that is being conducted by the Member States regarding the use of unmanned aircraft in the security field. Section 4 describes how drone surveillance activities can impact the privacy and data protection rights of citizens. Section 5 concludes by offering some recommendations regarding the general principles to be applied in the regulations governing the collection of personal data by drones for law enforcement purposes.

2. Definition and Uses of Drones

In a nutshell, the term drone is used to describe any type of aircraft that is piloted by remote control. These vehicles fly without the presence of a pilot on board and are remotely controlled from somewhere else (earth, space or another aircraft).[15] These remotely piloted aviation systems are the only ones that can be authorised nowadays for use in European airspace. Along with this type of drone, there are unmanned drones which are automatically programmed, but not remotely piloted, and are not yet authorised for use under ICAO or EU rules.

Drones are no longer used solely by the military. Manufacturers are now making a variety of them with different designs, sizes and functionalities to meet the specific needs of companies and customers. Drones are becoming in-

---

though its implications on the processing of personal data, its analysis isn't addressed in this paper as it is far from our scope. For this, see EDPS, *Recommendations on the proposed European Border and Coast Guard Regulation,* 18 March 2016, and RIJMA, J., *Study for the LIBE Committee on The proposal for a European Border and Coast Guard: evolution or revolution in external border management,* European Parliament, March 2016.

15. More precisely and according to ICAO, a drone is "a set of configurable elements consisting of a remotely-piloted aircraft, its associated remote pilot station(s), the required command and control links and any other system elements as may be required, at any point during flight operation" (Article 29 Data Protection Working Party, *Opinion 01/2015 on Privacy and Data Protection Issues relating to the Utilisation of Drones,* WP 231, 16 June 2015, p. 6).

creasingly cheaper, more capable of sustained flight, and offer a versatility of functions for carrying out activities considered unpleasant or difficult (the famous three Ds for "dirty, dull, and dangerous" tasks).

Drones that are used for civil or non-military activities can be classified according to the agents involved. This approach, in our view, is the most appropriate one for analysing the applicable legal regime.

First, companies and professionals use drones in large-scale infrastructures (bridges, plants, nuclear plants, railways, etc.) that take a variety of forms: agricultural management and crop monitoring, power line surveying, coverage of large public events, aerial photography, global environmental monitoring and security related operations, fire services, fisheries protection, oil and gas pipeline surveying, pizza delivery or books orders, and reporting of journalistic information.

Second, law enforcement uses also take a variety of forms: for example, search and rescue, disaster response, border patrols, civil protection, monitoring protests or crowded events, aerial surveillance, traffic management and monitoring, search and rescue, disposal of explosives, prevention or threats to public security, detection, observation and tracking-pursuit of criminal suspects, and observation of civil unrest, among others.

Third, private individuals use drones as hobbies, including model aircraft activities, as well as for photography and information technology. The use of drones for private activities deserves a brief comment. Article 2.2 GDPR recognizes a "domestic exemption" which excludes the processing of personal data from the scope of its application: "(c) by a natural person in the course of a purely personal or household activity." On the assumption that the main use of drones by private individuals involves leisure and entertainment, it therefore qualifies as part of an individual's private or family life, and there are no obligations under the Regulation. Thus, those who use drones only for personal use (e.g., photographs or recordings while practising sports or while enjoying family gatherings, etc.) fall outside the application of the GDPR. Otherwise, individuals who use drones to capture, process and record of images or data from identified and identifiable people must respect the principles and obligations set forth in the GPDR. For example, a very common case involves the use of drones by individuals for surveillance of private property when it involves constant monitoring affecting, even partially, public spaces.[16]

---

16. See the CJUE, 11 December 2014, case *Frantisek Rynes vs Czech Data Protection Authority*, (C-212/13). The Court ruled that surveillance carried out by "the operation of a camera system, as a result of which a video recording of people is stored on a continuous

3. Use of Drones for Law Enforcement in Europe

a. Use of drones in Member States for law enforcement purposes

The use of drones by law enforcement agencies in Europe has become very popular and we learn daily about state agencies in Member States using drones to monitor protests, control traffic, track down drivers who break traffic laws, fight crime by spying in the sky, and searching buildings in which marijuana is being grown, etc.

More specifically, the UAV CannaChoper is a drone that is being used to detect outdoor plantations of cannabis in *Switzerland* and the *Netherlands*. In the latter country, a drone supported the police during evictions at a squatter quarter in February 2008.[17] *France,*[18] *Italy,*[19] and the *UK*[20]have used drones to track down undocumented workers or illegal immigrants and other criminalized or marginalized groups, as well as to control traffic, demonstrations and riots.

UK is the most advanced European country in terms of using drones for law enforcement purposes. UK police have frequently used drones to monitor rock fans, as well as to enforce Anti-Social Behaviour Orders. Since March 2014, Sussex Police have been using an Aeryon Skyranger at Gatwick Airport. Currently, the Surrey and Sussex Police have the largest drone squadrons in the UK, and have trained 38 of their staff members regarding how to fly drones, including the following units: staff at Gatwick Airport, the armed response unit, the forensic collision investigation and reconstruction units, a targeted patrol team, a neighbourhood response team, and a command search and operations planning unit.

In *Germany,*[21] the German Federal Police have acquired Aladin and Fancopter drones that allow them to monitor smuggling in border areas and the

---

recording device such as a hard disk drive, installed by an individual on his family home for the purposes of protecting the property, health and life of the home owners, but which also monitors a public space, does not amount to the processing of data in the course of a purely personal or household activity, for the purposes of that provision." (para. 35).

15. EICK, V., "Drone War Is Coming Home: A View from across the Ocean", *Social Justice Debates,* 2 April 2013.

16. "France officials use drones for traffic control", 5 October 2015.

17. "Turin police use spies in the sky to fight crime", 1 April 2014.

18. "UK Police May Use Drones To Monitor Protests, Siege Operations", 1 May 2016.

19. "The dark side of drones: Big Brother in Germany's skies", 26 September 2012.

regional police forces of Saxony and North-Rhine Westphalia have used the AirRobot. But many other federal states have significant experience in using drones to conduct surveillance of certain groups of people, such as alleged hooligans in Saxony or protesters rallying against atomic waste transports in Lower-Saxony. Experts assume that almost all special law-enforcement units at the state level use unmanned aircraft to discreetly capture images during hostage situations or ransom deliveries.

In *Austria*,[22] the Defence Minister has declared that his nation would use drones for the purpose of conducting surveillance of areas surrounding Austrian soldiers on foreign lands. Additionally, drones are being used to prevent illegal immigration and to observe naturally dangerous areas such as snowy mountains in an effort to prevent natural disasters or, at the least, to try to ensure that all civilians caught within the scope of a disaster are evacuated.

Currently, *Portugal* is considering using drones to investigate and take action in the event of traffic accidents. In addition, in collaboration with several universities, Greek police have deployed drones for surveillance against forest fires and arson, and they are also using them against criminals and large demonstrations in Athens. Since 2014, when the massive migratory movements began, Greece has used drones to detect illegal immigrants crossing border points that are not accessible by border guards or other means.[23]

b. Use of drones in Spain for law enforcement purposes

Spain is a relative latecomer to the use of drones by state agencies but a study by the Spanish Centre for National Defence Studies[24] in 2012 suggested that drone technology has promising possibilities for law enforcement purposes, including uses by the coastguard, fire fighting, border patrol and law enforcement.

Since 2011, the *Mossos d'Esquadra*—the Catalonian Police—have used drone squadrons to receive and transmit signals in the search for missing persons. Since that time, new possibilities have been explored and a group of police officers have been trained. In 2015, the *Mossos* formed the first team of drone pilots certified by the Spanish Aviation Safety Agency. In May 2016, the team used these devices with infrared cameras to find cannabis farms.[25]

---

22. "Austrian military to use surveillance drones", 4 June 2012.
23. "Greece deploys drones to detect 'illegal immigrants' ", 11 October 2015.
24. Centro Superior de Estudios de la Defensa Nacional, *Los sistemas no tripulados*, Ministerio de Defensa, Madrid, 2012.
25. "Helicopters and drones fly over Spain to 'hunt' cannabis farms", 4 May 2016.

The *Guardia Civil*—a Spanish armed institute—announced, in 2013, that it would use drones for border and maritime surveillance in the framework of the CLOSEYE project. The Service for the Protection of the Nature (SEPRONA) has also used drones for the surveillance, and the prevention of fires, dumping and poaching.

In 2015, the National Police used a drone during the investigation of a fire at a factory in Burgos, taking aerial pictures and accessing areas where it was difficult to see. The aircraft was capable of reconstructing the fire scene in 3D and recreating its evolution, using hypotheses suggested by researchers.

More recently, in 2016, the National Department of Traffic tested a drone for traffic control in motorways, but Spanish regulation of drones (Act 18/2014, 15 October) does not permit development of this use since pilots may not fly drones beyond their visual line of sight. This limitation constitutes, at present, the main challenge to expanding police use of drones, and it is also hampered by a lack of specific standards and comprehensive regulation.

4. The Current European Data Protection Framework

a. Privacy and data protection concerns regarding the use of drones for surveillance

The use of drones can be both glorified and demonized. Even though virtually nobody would object to using drones to monitor chemical plants, or carry out searches for missing persons, many object when drones are used to constantly surveil properties and public spaces.

The advantages of drones are undeniable.[26] Drones can monitor large or inaccessible areas,[27] especially in the context of a search and rescue context in a dense forest or large coastline. They can also be used to prevent illegal immigration or human trafficking. Drones are also mobile which allows them to detect, register and track objects and individuals. Moreover, drones are less visible than CCTV cameras or other aircraft surveillance systems such as helicopters and they are more difficult to detect by potential wrongdoers.

26. VERMEULEN, M., *SURVEILLE Deliverable D4.7: The scope of the right to private life in public places*, 27 July 2014, pp. 6–7.

27. CLARKE, R., "What drones inherit from their ancestors", *Computer Law & Security Review*, n. 30, 2014, pp. 247–262.

From a privacy and data protection standpoint, the crucial issue is not the use of drones *per se* but the data processing equipment on-board drones, and the subsequent processing of personal data that may take place.[28] In this sense the key strength of drones is that they can be equipped with a large variety of technologies and capabilities, including simple onboard cameras and sensors to extreme complex technologies such as high-power zoom lenses, night vision, infrared, ultraviolet, thermal imaging, and radar technologies, video analytic technology, speakers capable of monitoring personal conversations, distributed video or facial and other soft biometric recognition.[29] As we have seen, these payloads allow police to take aerial photographs with high definition, for monitoring crowds at events such as protests or sporting, hacking WI-FI networks to intercept communications, the identification of criminals or the monitoring of the suspects, to mention just a few examples.

On the other hand, police and government non-military uses of drones have fueled public suspicion and controversy because of their potential impact on civil rights and liberties.[30] As the European Data Protection Supervisor (EDPS) warned, even if such tools can be instruments for legitimate (and regulated) use by law enforcement bodies or intelligence agencies, they can also be misused and have a negative impact on human rights, especially on the protection of personal data and privacy.[31] Drones can operate in public and semi-public places, with an impact on *behavioural privacy*, and their ability to avoid physical barriers such as fences or walls enables them to enter private spaces. Sometimes, drones are equipped with thermal sensors that can be used to detect human presence or movement, thereby affecting an individual's *privacy of location.*

The relative invisibility of drones has an impact on privacy as people often are unaware of whether they are being watched. Knowledge of the surveillance may produce a *panoptic or chilling effect* that encourages people to behave dif-

28. Article 29 Data Protection Working Party, *Opinion 01/2015 on Privacy and Data Protection Issues relating to the utilisation of drones*, cit., p. 7.

29. CLARKE, R., "Understanding the drone epidemic", *Computer Law & Security Review*, n. 30, 2014, pp. 230–246.

30. Another public concern is the extent to which law enforcement drones will be more similar to those designed for military or for civilian purposes. This appreciation comes from the perception that nations are adopting a more aggressive approach for police uses of drones and the common characteristics that law enforcement drones have with military facilities (CLARKE, R., "Understanding the drone epidemic", cit., p. 241).

31. EDPS, *Opinion 8/2015 on the Dissemination and use of intrusive surveillance technologies*, 15 December 2015.

ferently in order to comply with social or political conventions, and which may unduly inhibit them from exercising their legitimate civil rights. Indeed, knowledge of monitoring can seriously affect and undermine liberties such as freedom of expression and the right of association.[32] Invisibility of collection is also troublesome because there is the potential for the covert transmission of data collected by drones as images or recorded voices—data which can be transmitted online. This "double" invisibility can involve a risk to data protection as it can be difficult to meet *transparency, accountability and consent obligations*[33] and it makes harder for people to find out who is operating the drone and the purposes for which it is being used. Lack of transparency, along with the anonymity of those who conduct the surveillance, raise questions regarding how to enforce the rights of individuals, how to detect those responsible for surveillance, and how to require compliance with their duties to drones' operators or controllers. In addition, any error or abuse that may occur with drones is frequently ignored because data subjects may not be aware of the infringements to their privacy and data protection interests.

Access by law enforcement agencies to the large volumes of data collected by drones is of particular concern because massive amounts of personal data can be collected "not only for retrospective investigation, and not only once the fact of a criminal act is known or reasonable grounds for suspicion exist, but also prospectively, 'just-in-case.' "[34] As a result, the automated process of collecting data can create potential *purpose limitation* and *function* violations. The purpose limitation means that the data captured must be adequate, relevant, and not excessive in relation to the purposes for which it is being col-

32. For the notion of chilling effect on intellectual privacy, see COHEN, J. E., "What Privacy is For", *Harvard Law Review*, vol. 126, 2013, pp. 1904–1933.

33. FINN R. L, D. WRIGHT, A. DONOVAN, L. JACQUES and P. DE HERT, *Privacy, data protection and ethical risks in civil RPAS operations. D3.3: Final report for the European Commission*, 7 November 2014, p. 14.

34. CLARKE, R., "The regulation of civilian drones' impacts on behavioural privacy", *Computer Law & Security Review*, n. 30, 2014, p. 287. De Hert warns against the shift from a reactive to a pro-active security and crime policy based on "the use of data mining and post-hoc behavioural pattern analysis systems, whereby the use of ICT-based systems facilitates data collection and sharing between multiple sources in support of intelligence gathering" and the reinforcement of "the powers of governments and law enforcement bodies to access individuals' personal data for purposes different from those for which the data were originally gathered, supplied and processed." (DE HERT, P., "Balancing security and liberty within the European human rights framework. A critical reading of the Court's case law in the light of surveillance and criminal law enforcement strategies after 9/11", *Utrecht Law Review*, Volume 1, Issue 1, 2005, pp. 68–69).

lected and/or further processed. The risk of function creep is really high in the law enforcement sector where drones are purchased for precisely orientated uses, but may be used for other contested purposes. Even though, for example, drones might legitimately be used to detect illegal immigration on borders or at sea, there is a risk that they will also be misused to monitor minor or irrelevant events such as police monitoring of crowd gatherings or the detection of people who have not paid for parking.[35]

Last but not least, drones present an important challenge for *profiling*. Profiling involves "any form of automated processing of personal data consisting of the use of personal data to evaluate certain personal aspects relating to a natural person, in particular to analyse or predict aspects concerning that natural person's performance at work, economic situation, health, personal preferences, interests, reliability or behaviour, location or movements" (Article 4.4 GDPR). Profile techniques have been used in the public sector to predict a variety of risky patterns in the population and have encouraged appropriately focused actions by law enforcement agencies. As a perverse effect, profiling may lead to what is called "social sorting", that is, discrimination and stigmatization against specific individuals and social groups based upon flawed assumptions or even faulty statistical methods.

b. Lack of specific rules on drone technology

In Europe, both academics and lawmakers have wondered whether it is necessary to create privacy rules specifically for drone use rather than analysing drones under general privacy rules. In France and Hungary, governmental officials are in the process of preparing specific legislation governing the use of drones. The Hungarian Authority for Data Protection and Freedom of Information[36] released a document, concluding that the Privacy Act and existing international and European legislation on data protection are insufficient to address the current complexity of drone systems. In the Authority's view, the

35. FINN R. L, D. WRIGHT, A. DONOVAN, L. JACQUES and P. DE HERT, *Privacy, data protection and ethical risks in civil RPAS operations*, cit. Tom Barry, senior analyst at the Center of International Policy in Washington, offers another good example of function creep. He told that the US Department of Homeland Security had destined some civil drones to operate as instruments of border security but a number of these devices were quickly engaged in the "war of drugs" (BARRY, T., "Homeland Security Drones Mission Creep from Border Security to National Security", *Borderlines Blog*, March 2013).

36. National Authority for Data Protection and Freedom of Information of Hungary, *Opinion on Data Processing by Drones*, 2 April 2015, p. 7.

analogic application of regulations concerning other devices—such as surveillance cameras or aerial photographs—is not suitable to the data processing conducted by drones because they have special features which demand a separate set of regulations. These features come from the attributes of drones explained above (indiscernible, unregistered, mobile and small-sized aircraft) that cause them to differ from other technologies and allow them to exercise new and greater surveillance potentials (extensiveness, intensity, panoptic effect, surreptitious).

On the other hand, some countries such as Spain consider that the privacy issues relating to drones are sufficiently covered by existing laws, and that drone technology does not require the creation of new laws. The forthcoming Spanish regulation on the civil use of drones—now under preparation—does not include any specific provision relating to the protection of privacy and personal data. The operation of a drone by a state authority for purposes of search and surveillance is subject to the general provisions applicable to searching and wiretapping, and as supplemented by data protection provisions.

In the absence of specific regulation, or when states fail to adapt existing provisions, standards governing governmental use of drones have been left to the judiciary[37] and the courts. Indeed, courts at both the European and national levels, are in the process of addressing and updating the regulatory issues that drones raise in relation to security and surveillance.

In the European context, the judgements of the CJUE in *Digital Rights Ireland* and, more recently, in *Schrems* confirm the importance of a high level of protection, especially in connection with law enforcement and national security. In *Digital Rights Ireland*,[38] the Court held that the obligations imposed by the Directive on Data Retention constitutes an interference with the right to privacy as does the access of competent authorities to that data. In the *Schrems*[39] ruling, the Court held that the access of public authorities on a generalised basis to the content of electronic communications undermines the very essence of the right to privacy.[40] The Court also declared that mass surveillance is inherently a problem, irrespective of the safeguards put in place to limit its abuse. Specifically, the Court ruled that mass surveillance of the con-

---

37. The thesis that legislative regulation of drones is preferable to their regulation by the courts is developed in SMITH, M. L., "Regulating law enforcement's use of drones: the need for state legislation", *Harvard Journal on Legislation*, vol. 52, 2014, pp. 423–454.

38. Joined cases C-293/12 and C-594/12, *Digital Rights Ireland* and *Seitlinger*, ECLI:EU:C:2014/238.

39. Case C-362/14, *Schrems*, ECLI:EU:C:2015:650.

40. http://curia.europa.eu/jcms/upload/docs/application/pdf/2015-10/cp150117en.pdf

tent of communications breaches the essence of the right to privacy and cannot be justified. Surveillance of content, which is *targeted* at suspected criminal activities or security threats, is regarded as clearly justifiable.[41]

National courts are also making efforts to update their laws, and attaching present-day technological conditions on their legal frameworks. In Spain, the Supreme Court recently held that the police acted illegally in observing the interior of a home through binoculars without judicial permission. The Court warned that drones and other "intrusive devices" might infringe the inviolability of the home so that a "functional—not formalistic—interpretation" of constitutional provisions must be adopted.[42] The German Federal Court of Justice has stated that the same restrictions that civilian drones are subject to the same restrictions that apply to the use of GPS tracking devices to conduct surveillance. The court explained that there is a risk that civilian drones will use photography or film technology to severely breach the personality rights of those being watched.[43] Finally, an Administrative Court of Appeal in Sweden ruled that a drone equipped with a camera is subject to the rules relating to camera surveillance even if the camera can be used only for a short time in the air. The Court has accepted the argument of the Data Inspectorate that drone flight time is not crucial under the surveillance law.[44] The effect of these decisions is that private life and communications are protected from illegal intrusions by new technological devices, and that these devices and drones are fully subject to surveillance and data protection laws.

c. Regulatory questions regarding drones: data protection and surveillance legislation

The regulatory questions facing drones affect three different issues: first, the *technical requirements* imposed by the national aviation authorities; second, *data protection implications* when the drone is used to process personal data and, finally, *surveillance regulations*, that is, CCTV cameras, telecommunications and criminal laws.

Leaving aside aviation regulations regarding the use of drones, the legal framework on privacy and data processing and data handling in Europe is based on Convention 108 of the Council of Europe, Article 8 of the European Con-

41. PEERS, S., "The party's over: EU data protection law after the Schrems Safe Harbour judgment", *EU Law Analysis*, 7 October 2015.

42. Sentence of the Spanish Supreme Court 329/2016, 3 May, ECLI:ES:TS:2016:1709.

43. German Federal Court of Justice, 4 June 2013.

44. Administrative Court of Appeal in Jönköping, 21 December 2015.

vention of Human Rights, Articles 7 (privacy) and 8 (data protection) of the EU Charter of Fundamental Rights, as well as Article 16 TFUE and Directive 95/46 EC, to be replaced by the GDPR in May 2018.

The activities performed by drones for the purpose of handling and processing personal data must comply with the above-mentioned regulations and must respect the fundamental rights to privacy and data protection. The Opinion of the EDPS[45] underscores the fact that any interference with the exercise of these rights must be carried out in accordance with Article 8.2 ECHR (and Article 52.1 of the Charter). Consequently, these interferences must be developed in accordance with law, which must be made known to the public in such a way that they are informed about how their rights may be abridged, and they are able to foresee when they will likely be subjected to measures involving drones. The document also suggests that the methods and ways that drones are used by law enforcement authorities should not be secret and that their use should serve one of the legitimate goals set forth in the aforementioned Article 8.2 ECHR, and must be necessary in a democratic society, that is respond to a "pressing social need"? This expression can be translated into the requirement that drone use by law enforcement authorities in the context of a specific investigation must be proportionate, necessary and satisfy the requirement that there by no other less intrusive alternatives that would achieve the same purpose.

Examining the GDPR, the key principles regarding the processing of personal data include consent, lawfulness, fairness and transparency, purpose limitation, data minimisation, accuracy, security, storage limitation, integrity, confidentiality and accountability (Articles 5 to 7 GDPR). But this Regulation should not apply to processing activities for the purposes of the prevention, investigation, detection or prosecution of criminal offences or the execution of criminal penalties, including the safeguarding against and the prevention of threats to public security and the free movement of such data, as it is the subject of a specific Union legal act, namely Directive (EU) 2016/680 of the European Parliament and of the Council. The Police and Criminal Justice Data Protection Directive provides a harmonized framework for data processing activities with purposes of prevention, investigation, detection or prosecution of criminal offences and it is said to ease data exchanges by setting a common standard of data protection and to protect EU citizens against mass surveillance or indiscriminate bulk data collection.

45. EDPS, *Opinion on the Communication from the Commission to the European Parliament and the Council on "A new era for aviation—Opening the aviation market to the civil use of remotely piloted aircraft systems in a safe and sustainable manner"*, 26 November 2014.

However, this statement must be qualified in light of two elements. First, the subsidiarity of the GDPR. As the Regulation declares, Member States may entrust competent authorities within the meaning of Directive 2016/680 with tasks that are not necessarily carried out for the purposes described above. Coercive measures such as police activities at demonstrations, major sporting events or traffic control are examples of tasks that are not necessarily carried out for the purposes of preventing, investigating, detecting or prosecuting criminal offences "so that the processing of personal data for those other purposes, in so far as it is within the scope of Union law, *falls within the scope of this Regulation*".

Second, Article 23 GPDR recognizes national and public security; defence and state activities in the criminal area as a limit to its scope of application[46] but these restrictions are not absolute and have received strong criticism.

Thus, the EDPS has assessed the wording of this restriction negatively: "As far as the exception for 'activities falling outside the scope of Union law' is concerned, the EDPS wishes to express a more general comment. While 'national security' falls outside the scope of Union law, it is not always fully clear what this notion covers, as it depends on Member States national policy. At national level, the use of the wording 'national security' or 'state security', depending on Member States, with a different scope of application, can also be confusing. Obviously, the EDPS does not contest the exception, but he considers that it should be avoided that it is unduly used to legitimise the processing of personal data outside the scope of the Regulation and the Directive, for instance in the context of the fight against terrorism."[47]

We believe that some special conditions and accommodation must be imposed in certain activities or areas. In this sense, the provisions covering law enforcement agencies regarding security and criminal matters may include exemptions to the scope or principles of Data Protection regulation as far as the

46. Article 23 GDPR. *Restrictions* "1. Union or Member State law to which the data controller or processor is subject may restrict by way of a legislative measure the scope of the obligations and rights provided for in Articles 12 to 22 and Article 34, as well as Article 5 in so far as its provisions correspond to the rights and obligations provided for in Articles 12 to 22, when such a restriction respects the essence of the fundamental rights and freedoms and is a necessary and proportionate measure in a democratic society to safeguard: (a) national security; (b) defence; (c) public security (d) the prevention, investigation, detection or prosecution of criminal offences or the execution of criminal penalties, including the safeguarding against and the prevention of threats to public security; (...)".

47. EDPS, *Opinion of the European Data Protection Supervisor on the Data protection reform package*, 7 March 2012, p. 15.

derogations are justified, adequate and proportionate to the objective in view.[48] Police may need to save data over long periods and make links between different criminal offences detected seem irrelevant when they are detected for the first time. Also persons suspected of having committed a crime may not have access to their files or even be informed that they are under investigation by the police until they have been charged with an offence.

Finally, and in order to complete the legal scenario, security and surveillance are primarily an issue for Member States and therefore, there is a vast range of regulatory instruments that have been introduced in individual countries. Although some regulation regarding security can be found in the EU context, covering particular policy areas (such as aviation, border control and cybercrime), the landscape regarding surveillance regulation is very complex and extensive.

If we focus our attention on the use of drones by state agencies, we see that they are subject to two different regimes at the national level: the national data protection law when they process personal data and the surveillance regulations on the law enforcement sector (surveillance cameras, surveillance of telecommunications and Criminal Procedure Codes). The analysis of national privacy and surveillance regimes in the European Commission study[49] concludes that such legislation is right now, focused on "classical" forms of surveillance—such as interception of communications and the capture of images—but do not include the capabilities that new technologies provide (geolocalisation, data bulking, biometric data, etc.). Likewise, the fragmentation of surveillance regimes and the lack of harmonisation between the Member States may provide insufficient safeguards for privacy and data protection. Nevertheless, many countries have declared that the regulation applicable to CCTV is applicable to drones as well. Although this isn't the most desirable approach, it is acceptable because in most of these countries general rules on privacy and data protection apply to CCTV.[50] This is the case in Denmark, Finland, France, Italy, Germany and Spain.

Member States' data protection laws exempt the processing of personal data carried out by public authorities in security and criminal areas from nearly all

48. DE HERT, P. and V. PAPAKONSTANTINOU, "The Police and Criminal Justice Data Protection Directive: Comment and Analysis", *Computers & Law Magazine of SCK*, vol. 22, Issue 6, 2012, pp. 1–5.

49. FINN R. L, D. WRIGHT, A. DONOVAN, L. JACQUES and P. DE HERT, *Privacy, data protection and ethical risks in civil RPAS operations*, cit.

50. An overview of national regulations regarding CCTV and Data Protection issues in VOISIN, V., "Unmanned Aerial Systems: Privacy and Regulatory Implications across Europe, the Middle East and Asia-Pacific", 1 March 2016.

data protection provisions affecting individual's rights, fundamental data protection principles or the obligation to notify prior to review by the Data Protection Authority. This is the common situation across Europe. These exemptions, which are based in domestic laws, have been criticised because "they are too broad and provide blanket exemption (not given on a case-by-case basis)" and certain provisions are even unjustified, for example the obligation to notify the Data Protection Authority and the prior checking mechanism: "Consequently, data protection risks raised by the RPAS when they are used by State agencies for processing personal data in relation to national security or criminal area will not be adequately mitigate by national data protection law".[51]

5. General Principles to Be Met on the Use of Personal Data Collected by Means of Drones for Law Enforcement Purposes

The unstoppable development of drone technology will be certainly exploited by law enforcement agencies through expanded use. Only a few Member States are currently adapting their legislation on data protection to the specific use of drones. These national legislations, and any other future proposals, must meet several general principles.

The requirements for data processing by the police and any other law enforcement authorities using drones must have a legal basis, and be permissible under the principles detailed below. They are cumulative, not alternative, and any conflation of these principles must be avoided.

1. *Necessity*: the processing of data for government use must be done in compliance with the rules on necessity. The adaption of this requirement for police and security forces means that data pooling and data processing for observation or for a possibility thereof, may not be allowed. This rule is especially binding in cases involving data processing for criminal purposes, as data processing may only be used for individual cases and in compliance with the rules on criminal proceedings, including the requirement of a previous judicial authorisation.

2. ***Proportionality***: the use of drones for processing data is governed by the principle of proportionality, both in terms of appropriateness and minimal intervention. This means that the impact on privacy must be proportionate with

51. *Ibid.*, p. 320.

the expected benefits and authorities must show why there is no satisfactory alternative that will achieve their purposes but have a smaller impact on privacy. When an alternative will be as effective, but have a lesser impact on privacy, the police or law enforcement agency should use that alternative. In criminal investigations and law enforcement activities one shall always assess an activity's impact on the privacy of innocent (not suspected) persons, and select the method with the smallest impact on those persons.[52] The Privacy Impact Assessment (PIAs) is a proactive technique which assists organisations in assessing (identifying and minimising) the privacy risks of new projects or policies. This measure was included in Article 35 GDPR and is very important for drone operations, as they are likely to result in significant risks to the rights and freedoms of natural persons. The outcome of the assessment should be taken into account by law enforcement agencies in determining the appropriate measures to be taken in order to mitigate risks.[53]

3. ***Purpose limitation***: personal data must be collected for specified, explicit and legitimate purposes and not further processed in a way incompatible with those purposes. In addition, the purpose limitation must be observed throughout the entire data processing. Data processing for government purposes must also comply with this principle and, for instance, aerial images taken for the protection of historic sites may not include the data of people walking by or vehicles in circulation. When images must be taken of a catastrophic area, the drone must not record during the way to or back from the area. Besides, the recordings shall not be processed for other purposes such as the creation of databases and they must not be transferred.

4. ***Transparency principle:*** Data processing should be transparent to data subjects. As much as possible, subjects should be informed of the processing as well as regarding their rights. Any refusal to provide information or any restriction of the right to information is only permissible in situations defined in the legislation and in individual cases.

Nevertheless, there are special conditions on the principle of transparency and the obligation to provide information when the surveillance measures are being conducted by law enforcement agencies, which may have a need for secrecy regarding certain activities (e.g. the actual surveillance of specific persons). In this context, transparency applies to the way in which decisions are

---

52. National Authority for Data Protection and Freedom of Information of Hungary, *Opinion on Data Processing by Drones*, cit.

53. For an example, see U.S. Department of Homeland Security, *Privacy Impact Assessment for the Aircraft Systems*, 9 September 2013.

reached, and the principles underlying such decisions, but not to transparency regarding concrete measures. The duty to notify individuals must be performed within a reasonable time after the surveillance operation.

5. ***Retention period:*** Data processing by drones must be carried out within a specific procedure for which there is a legal basis, especially when it affects a particular group of persons, and must not be performed in a pooling manner that targets large crowds of people with a general purpose. Any legal provision enabling data collection and processing for another purpose shall incorporate appropriate guarantees and limitations regarding access to and use of such data.

6. ***No indiscriminate surveillance:*** Law enforcement data processing carried out by means of drones should not involve the constant tracking of individuals. If constant tracking is found to be strictly necessary, it must be restricted to law enforcement warranted investigations.

7. ***Prohibition of automated enforcement of decisions***: One concern regarding the use of drones by police and state agents, including the military use, is the risk of dehumanisation of decisions since the agent is far away from his objective and this physical distance may weaken the constraints of conscience. To avoid this problem, a prohibition against automated enforcement of decisions should apply to these uses. The data processed via drones should be further scrutinised by a human operator before any decision is taken which adversely affects an individual.

8. ***Revision by courts and special regime of approval.*** Judicial power must extend to the use of drones for law enforcement purposes in order to ensure that all principles and requirements have been observed. In addition, the use of drones for law enforcement, even in case of warranted investigations, such as targeted surveillance, should require a sufficiently high-level approval in the organisational hierarchy.

9. ***Solutions based in technology (privacy by design and by default principles).*** Although focused on manufacturers, the so-called Privacy Enhancing Technologies (PETs) can also be a positive instrument for ensuring that breaches of the data protection rules are forbidden and made technically more difficult. Article 25 GDPR incorporates privacy by design and by default which are technical solutions that may appropriately cover the data protection risks of drones as a surveillance technology. For example, by providing tools with data protection friendly functionalities, such as the possibility to turn on and off sensors in flight, and avoiding permanent recording of images and data, provide significant protections. This functionality prevent law enforcement drones from gathering excessive images and videos to achieve their stated purposes.

In the process of adapting to a new regulatory context, Data Protection Authorities are contributing to a fair use of drones in private, commercial and state uses by adopting guides regarding the use of unmanned aircrafts. These guides provide information about the impact of data protection regulation on drones' activities, and issue guidance suggesting that drones fitted with cameras do come under the auspices of data protection law.

In July 2015, the Information Commissioner of the Republic of Slovenia issued a report of the use of drones in relation to the Data Protection Acts.[54] In the UK, the Information Commissioner Officer (ICO) has recently revised the Code of Practice on CCTV to incorporate drone technology.[55] The Commission Nationale de l'Informatique et des Libertés (CNIL) in France has published several articles focused on the use of drones and video surveillance.[56] Also the Belgian Privacy Commission is offering information on its web page under the format of FAQs related to the use of drones.[57] The Czech Data Protection Authority issued its Position num. 1/2013 which adresses the processing of personal data gathered by drones.[58] The Irish Data Protection Commissioner is the last authority that has produced and issued new guidance on the use of drones in relation to the Data Protection Act in Ireland.[59]

6. Conclusions

The use of drones has crossed from the military to the civilian world, and the use of drone devices by law enforcement authorities is increasingly spreading throughout Europe. The trio of "surveillance-cameras–air" has proved very effective for national security, defence, public order and crime purposes. But the regulatory framework is really complex since it involves three different regimes: first, the technical requirements imposed by the national aviation authority; second, the *data protection implications* when the drone is processing

54. IPRS, *Unmanned aerial vehicles*, 30 July 2015.

55. ICO, *In the picture: A data protection code of practice for surveillance cameras and personal information*, Version 1.1, 21 May 2015.

56. CNIL, *Usages des drones et protection des données personnelles*, 30 October 2012; *Drones: quelle visión prospective, quels enjeux pour les libertés?*, 6 December 2013.

57. Commission for the Protection of Privacy, *Privacy Commission responds about drones. FAQ section.*

58. The Czech Office for Personal Data Protection, *Position No. 1/2013, Processing of personal data via recordings from cameras on unmanned aircraft*, January 2013.

59. DPC, *Guidance on the use of drones*, 25 December 2015.

personal data; and, finally, *surveillance regulations*, that is, CCTV cameras, telecommunications and criminal laws.

This article reveals that the security concept is being interpreted in such a broad sense that it allows national legislation to evade provisions on privacy and data protection. Besides, national surveillance laws are only focused on traditional forms of surveillance leaving unregulated the capabilities of new technologies. In many cases, the determination of standards for governmental drone use is left to the judiciary through the analogic application of legal provisions on video cameras.

But these solutions have proven to be incomplete and imprecise, and some European countries are moving toward the development of specific legal standards. This is also our position regarding upcoming legislation concerning the authorisation regime and data protection issues relating to the use of drones by law enforcement officers. We recommend inclusion of the key principles inspired by the GDPR, basically, which impose the following requirements: the need for a valid and legal ground purpose for the processing; processing only for a particular purpose within the necessary extent and only for a limited period; fulfilling transparency and notification obligations towards the data subjects; a prohibition against indiscriminate surveillance and automated enforcement decisions; review by courts and implementation of PIAs and PETs.

Rosario Serra-Cristóbal[1]

Surveillance on Data and Electronic Communications in the Counter-Terrorism Fight in Spain[2]

Abstract: The purpose of this essay is to highlight the necessity to respect both commonly accepted principles governing data processing and the rule of law when government's monitor communications and data in an effort to fight terrorism. From this perspective the essay analyses whether due guarantees are observed by the newly adopted Spanish 2015 legal framework on electronic surveillance.

1. Need for Surveillance of Data and Communications in the Fight against Terrorism

Spain, like many other countries, has been a target of Jihadist attacks.[3] The 2004 Madrid blasts caused 191 deaths and injured more than 2000 people.[4] It was one of the deadliest Jihadist attacks since 9/11. However, that attack was

1. Associated Professor of Constitutional Law, University of Valencia

2. This essay was realized in the framework of the R&D Group "Global Security and Fundamental Rights: the Protection Against Threats and the Guarantees of Liberties," defrayed by Spanish Ministry of Economy and Competitiveness (Ref. DER2015-65288-R).

3. Only as a mere example, recently, the ISIS widespread a propaganda video clip where the organisation said: "We will recover our land from the invaders," referring to past centuries when part of the Iberian Peninsula was occupied by Muslims.

4. These were not the first Jihadists attacks in Spain. On April 12, 1985 a terrorist attack occurred in the restaurant "El Descanso" of Madrid, claimed by a group of Islamic Jihad. 18 people died and over 100 were injured. The restaurant was frequented by US military although all the dead were Spanish. And the presence of radical Islamic networks on Spain can be traced back a decade prior to the attacks on Madrid in 2004. See Jordan, Javier and Horsburgh, Nicola (2005), "Mapping Jihadist Terrorism in Spain," *Studies in Conflict and Terrorism*, n. May.

followed by the attacks in London in 2005, in Paris in January 2015, in Copenhagen in 2015, in Paris again in November 2015, in Brussels in March 2016, as well as many other places around the world. The Paris assaults provoked a new and stronger public outcry, opening a new chapter in the fight against terrorism in the European Union. As a result, most nations have recognized a genuine need to increase homeland security and fight international terrorism.

Among the methods used to struggle terrorism, some have involved efforts to monitor data and electronic communications. As in other parts of the world, after Jihadist terrorist attacks, EU governments have pressed for more power to gather intelligence, not only from phone calls, but also from digital mass media such as Internet websites and social networks.[3]

Much information regarding terrorist groups can be obtained from Internet and from open sources such as web pages (open sources), but some can only be found though non-open sources (e.g., emails, financial transactions, Facebook). It is through these electronic frameworks that international terrorist organizations raise funds for attacks, seek supporters, defend their causes, coordinate groups, and mount terrorist attacks.[4]

As terrorists make use of the digital era's tools,[5] governmental monitoring and supervision of digital communications and data can be justified. Indeed, governments have great need to obtain information about both ISIS's members and their activities. Nevertheless, sometimes this is not enough. For instance, at least seven of the suspects involved in the planning and/or execution of the 2005 Madrid train bombings were already under police surveillance on suspicion of involvement in terrorism prior to the March 11 attack. Regard-

---

5. France adopted a new Act on intelligence services in 2015, that gives French intelligence services sweeping new spying abilities. Notwithstanding, the Constitutional Council struck down a provision from this Act that allowed intelligence services to conduct spying operations in emergency situations without referring to the commission or getting authorization from the Prime Minister. The provision was a "clearly disproportionate breach of the right to the respect of privacy and of the secret of correspondences," the Council said in a statement. It also quashed a provision that allowed intelligence services to spy on communications sent to or received from abroad because the conditions for its use were not sufficiently clear (Conseil Constitutionnel, Décision nº 2015-713 DC du 23 julliet 2015).

6. See, Brown, Ian y Korff, Douwe (2009), "Terrorism and the proportionality of Internet Surveillance," *European Journal of Criminology*, vol. 6 (2), p. 119

7. Daesh's activities constitute a new kind of terrorism: its members operate through a dispersed structure with a high degree of fanaticism, which facilitates immolations that cause widespread damages; it uses new tools for the financing and recruitment of its members such as social networks; it is difficult to pursue, it is like an invisible enemy that can appear as an isolated cell anywhere and in any city.

less, innovative technologies for processing and analysing "big data" offer new surveillance opportunities for national security agencies. Their use could help in the prosecution of terrorism and the search for potential terrorists, thereby helping prevent new acts of terror.

Today, it is technically possible to intercept telephone and electronic communications that take place anywhere in the world. The problem is that the control and collection of such information appears to be increasingly incisive (data are collected and evaluated with perspective, mapping people[8]), and is conducted in a global manner (millions of citizens are under surveillance) without adequate controls. Snowden's disclosure of U.S. National Security Agency (NSA) information revealed a vast surveillance operation that was infinitely larger than prior telecommunications surveillance operations.[9] The Snowden revelations provoked a collective outrage in Spain when it was revealed that a massive amount of communications involving Spanish citizens had also been tracked by the NSA. Indignation became confusion when the NSA director declared that national intelligence services from allied countries, including Spain, had provided such information as part of their joint effort to guarantee common security.[10] Nevertheless, the surveillance capacities of the Spanish government (in terms of budget, technology and human resources) was low in comparison to the magnitude of the operations launched by British Intelligence Services (GCHQ) and the NSA.

There is a significant risk that these massive counter-terrorism operations could erode fundamental rights protected by the international framework, as well as by domestic constitutions, including the right to intimacy, secrecy of communications, and the right to self-determination regarding our data. Actually, those rights are guaranteed by Article 18 of the Spanish Constitution. Focused surveillance for criminal investigation purposes can be legitimate if

---

8. These data, once intercepted, are filtered and the suspicious ones are retained for further purposes.

9. They revealed that the US authorities were accessing and processing personal data of EU citizens on a large scale via, among others, the NSA's warrantless wiretapping of cable- bound internet traffic (UPSTREAM) and direct access to the personal data stored in the servers of US-based private companies such as Microsoft, Yahoo, Google, Apple, Facebook and Skype2 (PRISM). This allowed the US authorities to access both stored communications as well as to perform real-time collection on targeted users, through cross-database search programmes such as X-KEYSCORE.3 UPSTREAM, PRISM and X-KEYSCORE are only three of the most publicised programmes and represent the tip of the iceberg of the NSA's surveillance.

10. See, among others, the piece of news, Whitehead, Tom: "Germany, France and Spain 'were all spying on citizens'," *The Telegraph*, November 1, 2013.

framed consistently with the rule of law. However, large-scale surveillance with unclear objectives, which is loosely justified on national security grounds, could be a threat to individual rights.[11]

2. Electronic Surveillance to Fight against Foreign Terrorists

State concerns regarding terrorism have only increased with revelations regarding the online recruitment of potential Jihadist terrorist fighters. Europol reports that, in 2014, 395 persons were arrested for terrorist activities. In Spain, the country that is third in regard to detentions, the majority of the 34 detainees were accused of recruitment of potential terrorist fighters, and 45% of those arrested had Spanish nationality. Spain is considered a hotbed of Jihadist recruitment, with many new combatants coming out of the cities of Ceuta and Melilla (sited in North Africa).[12]

Such concerns underlie adoption of the U.N. Security Council Resolution 2178(2014) on Foreign Terrorist Fighters[13] and the general call for granting more data surveillance authority to intelligence agencies. In the Declaration of the Presidency of the Security Council of November 19, 2014[14] on "Threats to international peace and security caused by terrorist acts," the Security Council reiterated "its call on Member States to make use of the Interpol databases and to require that airlines under their jurisdiction provide advance passenger information to detect the departure from, entry into, or transit through their territories of individuals on the Al-Qaida sanctions list, and additionally encourages that they provide Passenger Name Records, where appropriate, to the appropriate national authorities."

---

11. The same point of view could be see in the study: BIGO, Diddier and others (2013): *National Programmes for mass surveillance of personal data in EU Member States and their compatibility with EU Law*, Brussels, European Parliament.

12. Ortega Dolz, Patricia: "45% of Jihadist arrested in Spain since 2013 are Spanish nationals," *El País*, November 16, 2015.

13. They are nationals traveling or attempting to travel to a State other than their State of residence or nationality, and others who travel or attempt to travel from their territories to a State other than their State of residence or nationality, with the purpose of committing, planning or preparing terrorist acts or participate in, or providing or receiving training for terrorist purposes." U.N. Security Council Resolution 2178(2014) on Foreign Terrorist Fighters, S/RES/2178 (2014)

14. S/PRST/2014/23.

On the basis of these international provisions and following Jihadist attacks in Paris (2015) and Brussels (2016), the EU reached agreements on data transfer that had been long debated, including the Directive regulating the use of Passenger Name Record (PNR) data in the EU for the prevention, detection, investigation and prosecution of terrorist offences and serious crime that was adopted on 21 April 2016. The implementation of this Directive requires that a set of data be generated for each passenger (name, address, itinerary, method of payment, number of bank cards, phone numbers, baggage information, travel dates, frequent flyer, travel agency, number and names of other travellers on the booking …) and that it be transmitted to the authorities. One can only wonder how Spain, as well as the other countries, will implement this obligation while respecting the privacy rights of European citizens.

Based on concerns about foreign terrorist fighters, the European Commission adopted a proposal for a Directive of the European Parliament and of the Council on combating terrorism.[15] Likewise, as a consequence of the necessity for improving counter-terrorism cooperation, a new legislative package updated and reinforced existing rules on data processing by means of two instruments: the General Data Protection Regulation 2016/679[16] (that replaces Directive 95/46/EC) and the Data Protection Directive in the area of Law Enforcement 2016/680 (that replaces Decision 2008/977/JHA).[17] Both the Regulation and the Directive will become applicable as of May 2018. The Regulation will "not be applied to the processing of personal data … in the course of an activity which falls outside the scope of the Union law, in particular concerning national security (or) by competent authorities for the purposes of prevention, investigation, detection or prosecution of criminal offences or the execution of criminal penalties." As a con-

15. Proposal for a Directive of the European Parliament and of the Council on combating terrorism and replacing Council Framework Decision 2002/475/JHA on combating terrorism. COM (2015) 625 final, 2015/0281 (COD) Brussels, 2.12.2015.

16. The Regulation (EU) 2016/679 of the European Parliament and of the Council of 27 April 2016 on the protection of natural persons with regard to the processing of personal data and on the free movement of such data, and repealing Directive 95/46/EC (General Data Protection Regulation), entered into force on 24 May 2016 and it shall apply from 25 May 2018.

17. Directive (EU) 2016/680 of the European Parliament and of the Council of 27 April 2016 on the protection of natural persons with regard to the processing of personal data by competent authorities for the purposes of the prevention, investigation, detection or prosecution of criminal offences or the execution of criminal penalties, and on the free movement of such data, and repealing Council Framework Decision 2008/977/JHA, entered into force on 5 May 2016 and EU Member States have to transpose it into their national law by 6 May 2018.

sequence, the framework applied to data flow in the areas of judicial and police cooperation in criminal matters is based on the aforementioned Directive.

The struggle against the phenomenon of foreign terrorist fighters in Spain prompted the Parliament to create new types of offenses for inclusion in the Criminal Code (Código Penal, CP). The Organic Act 2/2015 now penalizes those who are trained or receive indoctrination regarding the carrying out of terrorist offenses (Article 575), as well as individuals who regularly access communication services available to the public through the Internet that are designed to encourage the incorporation of a terrorist organization or collaborate with it, and, equally, any individual who moves to a Jihadist territory to collaborate with the terrorist movement.

3. Spanish Provisions on Exceptional Situations Related to Terrorism

Although Spain has been suffering from Basque ETA terrorist attacks for decades, it never felt the need to adopt a special statute on terrorism. Moreover, there was no effort to revamp laws in the aftermath of the Madrid trains bombing (2004), and no emergency legislation was sought as a consequence of these terrorist attacks.[18]

Recently, however, a new Act on National Security was approved (Act 36/2015 of National Security of September 28). Although the law does not specifically focus on terrorism, it does provide, for the first time, for a standard concept of national security, namely a State action "aimed at protecting freedom, rights and welfare of citizens, to ensure the defence of Spain and its constitutional principles and values, and to contribute with our partners and allies to international security in compliance with the commitments" (Article 3). It also states in its preamble that "Security is the foundation upon which a society may develop, preserve its freedom and prosperity of its citizens, and it ensures stability and proper functioning of its institutions." However, it does not create too many exceptions regarding fundamental rights. The Act focuses on risks and threats to the security of Spain, but does not expressly mention terrorism (yes to cybersecurity). However, the Act does refer to the National

---

18. See more in Beckman, James (2007), *Comparative Legal Approaches to Homeland Security and Anti-Terrorism*, Ashgate, pp. 118 and following.

Security Strategy of 2013,[19] where terrorism and cybercrime are considered as two of the risks and threats to national security.

Therefore, in the absence of specific legislation regarding terrorism, one must examine the various general statutes regarding security and rights for limitations on governmental authority. The provided limitations should be considered as exceptions to the general rules on fundamental rights. These provisions, derived from the Constitution, refer to certain rights accorded to investigated terrorists as a situation of exceptionality. In this context, the Act on criminal procedure (Ley de Enjuiciamiento Criminal, LEC) establishes the powers of law enforcement agencies and judicial authorities when conducting criminal investigations of terrorism, and their limits, while at the same time identifying the rights of terrorist suspects.

The terrorist attacks in Europe show that constitutional texts are not suited to deal with exceptional situations such as Jihadist terrorist assaults. The European states of emergency acts are not prepared in such a way that they are capable of reacting against terrorism in a balanced way. The situation is difficult because we are faced with terrorism that flows from unanticipated places, is carried out by subjects that can be located anywhere in the world, and uses new mechanisms.[20] The reaction to these attacks takes the shape of "state of emergency" declarations, as in France or Belgium among others. France even tried to alter its Constitution in order to reinforce governmental powers during states of emergency, but the amendment was not finally adopted.

In Spain, the general state of emergency provided for in the Constitution was not invoked after terrorist attacks.[21] Instead, the government ordered individual exceptional rights limitations for presumed terrorists. The Spanish Constitution is one of the few that provide for the suspension of individual rights for persons under investigation for belonging to terrorist organizations,

---

19. The Spanish government approved the National Security Strategy in May 2013, the first of its kind in Spain. The plan is driven by the Security Defence Committee, that is formed by representatives of various centres and agencies, including the National Centre of Intelligence, from different ministries.

20. Giuseppe de Vergottini (2004), "La difícil convivencia entre libertad y seguridad. Respuestas de las democracias al terrorismo" [Difficulties in the coexistence between liberty and security], *Revista de Derecho Político*, n. 61, p. 24.

21. Government used administrative mechanisms affecting security forces. Spain has been maintaining on a level 4 alert several times recently. A level 4 alert entails a strong presence of security personnel at strategic locations such as airports, train stations, power stations and telecommunications centres. All counter-terrorism units in police agencies have been activated. For now, however, the military has not been mobilized.

albeit always accompanied by a judicial warrant and other constitutional guarantees (Article 55.2 Spanish Constitution).[22] It is a provision designed to combat domestic terrorism (ETA), but it can be regarded as referring to any other type of terrorism.

The Constitution provides that extraordinary limits on a terrorist's rights can only be stated by Organic Act (a type of Act that requires the approval of more than half of the elected Parliament "Deputies") and it must relate to surveillance of presumed terrorist or persons being investigated for terrorism.

The government may adopt exceptional measures in the investigation of terrorism pursuant to the Act governing the Criminal Process (mentioned above), recently modified by Organic Act 13/2015 of October 5 to strengthen procedural measures in technological investigations. Apart from the special legal provisions for those accused of terrorism,[23] this essay will focus hereafter on those legal novelties related to cyber-surveillance in terrorist investigations.

4. New Spanish Legal Provisions on Cyber-Surveillance

In Spain, when collecting communications data that may affect secrecy (telephone or electronic wiretaps), the 1978 Constitution requires a court order, without distinguishing between type of communications or bulk surveillance of communications (Article 18.3).

When wiretaps are carried out by intelligence services, as part of their duties, the law is more ambiguous. However, the intelligence services are required to observe the provisions of the Organic Act 2/2002, providing for prior judicial control of the National Intelligence Centre. In particular, the Secretary of State, acting as Director of the National Centre of intelligence, must request

---

22. Article 55.2 reads "an Organic Act may determine the manner and the circumstances in which, on an individual basis and with the necessary participation of the courts and proper parliamentary control, the rights recognized in article 17, section 2 (*maximum period for preventive arrest*), and 18, sections 2 and 3 (*inviolability of home and secret of communications*), may be suspended for specific persons in connection with investigations of the activities of armed bands or terrorist groups.

Unwarranted or abusive use of the powers recognized in the foregoing organic act shall give rise to criminal liability as a violation of the rights and freedoms recognized by the laws."

23. The main features of Spain's counter-terrorism provisions are the extended period of detention in police custody allowed before the detainee must be brought before a judge (48 hrs. more), and the use of incommunicado detention.

the competent Justice of the Supreme Court for authorization to adoption measures affecting home inviolability and secrecy of communications. Since the intelligence service activities are covered by secrecy, it is difficult to know or control whether they respect due guarantees for fundamental rights in performing their duties.

It is not easy for citizens to know much about the types of investigations being performed by intelligence services. Moreover, in many of these operations, secrecy is crucial. However, when the scope of some intelligence operations have been publicly revealed, concerns have been voiced. For instance, there was controversy regarding SITEL wiretaps. SITEL is the system used by law enforcement authorities and operatives from the Spanish National Intelligence Centre which allows governmental officials to intercept and record in real time any phone call, email or phone message, and to store digital data regarding all such communications for further analysis.[24] Nonetheless, this advanced monitoring system may only be used with prior judicial authorization.

Apart from the above-cited constitutional provisions on wiretaps, and the scarce provisions governing oversight performed by intelligence services, no other regulation exists for controlling when and how government collects electronic communications and data. The law simply establishes certain general rules on data protection and imposes limitations on police officers when storing data during searches (Data Protection Organic Act 15/1999).[25]

This legal gap was filled by the provisions of the new Spanish Act governing the criminal process.[26] The Act was amended by the Organic Act 13/2015 to strengthen procedural protections and to regulate technological research measures. Included in the new articles are provisions for overseeing electronic communications, PCs, USBs, etc., which are regulated for the first time.

As a general rule, cyber-surveillance is only permitted when the government is investigating terrorism (or other serious crimes) and the Act almost always

24. A technical description of this system can be found in the Judgement of the Spanish Supreme Court 250/2009, of March 13, (F. J. 6)

25. The Data Protection Organic Act 15/1999 establishes that the collection and processing of sensitive or protected data may be made by the security forces without the consent of the holder, only in cases where it is absolutely necessary for the purposes of a specific investigation, and they should erase the data when it is no longer needed. The data may be kept if there exist dangers that could arise in the defence of the state, or for public safety, protection of rights and freedoms of others or the needs of the research being done.

26. The Act was amended recently to strengthen procedural measures and to regulate technological research measures (Act 13/2015, October 5).

requires a judicial warrant as a condition of such surveillance. Moreover, the new law includes a large list of requirements that must be satisfied in order to obtain a judicial warrant, and it requires that the judicial decision contain an extended discussion regarding the motivation for issuing the warrant.

The amended legislation imposes certain requirements on the government regarding the interception of electronic communications, USB devices, tracking and tracing devices, or remote logs of computer equipment (Article 588bis.a), including the following:

a) Speciality: The surveillance must be related to the investigation of a particular crime, and no surveillance may be authorized to prevent or discover crime, or investigate suspicions of terrorism, without an adequate factual basis. According to the explanatory statement, *a priori*, the Act prohibits measures involving prospective technological research.[27]

The ECHR demands legal authorization for strategic wiretapping (prospective), and the law must be respectful of fundamental rights. Proactive and preventive intelligence actions are necessary tools. Since terrorists operate in an electronic environment, attracting and securing communications and electronic data processing is crucial.[28] But everything must be done consistently with the rule of law and in the least invasive manner for individual rights.

b) Suitability: this requirement means that the government must define the objective and subjective scope and duration of the measure.

c) Exceptionality and necessity: The principle of necessity requires that surveillance can be done, and data processed, only if the measures taken are adequate, relevant and not excessive. In each case, it is necessary to determine whether we are collecting and processing data that relates to an adequate and relevant purpose. Such surveillance should be regarded as exceptional. Time should be taken to consider alternatives and less invasive counter-terrorism measures.

27. See Constitutional Court Judgment 253/2006.

28. Article 8.2 ECHR states that there shall be no interference of powers in the right to privacy and the confidentiality of correspondence and communications, as long as this interference is not provided for by law and is necessary to achieve one of the objectives of general interest, like national security. Therefore, the collection and processing of personal data and communications should occur only when it is really relevant to safeguard security. The notion of "necessity" is construed as a direct link between knowledge of this information and the defence of security in some specific aspect (see also Articles 4 and 8 of the new EU Directive on personal data).

d) Proportionality: This principle requires a balancing of two interests: security vs. privacy. The intervention must be carried out without unduly prejudicing the rights and freedoms of citizens. The balancing should consider whether there is a way to minimize the inevitable damage caused by cyber-surveillance in the fight against counter-terrorism. For instance, the decision-maker should consider whether a serious danger of terrorist attack exists, the consequences of non-intervention, the pre-existing evidence against certain individuals, and the utility of the data and communication's control, etc.

5. Interception of Phone Calls and Digital Communications

These type of actions may only be performed when investigating serious crimes under Article 579 of the Criminal Code, such as terrorism, and other crimes committed using electronic or communication means.

In principle, the law requires a judicial warrant in order to access the content of communications and electronic data (name of the correspondents, mobile numbers, etc.) or any other information related to communications. So, the judicial authorisation may cover many issues. The police may use technical devices to discover the IP address, IMSI or IMEI numbering or elements that identify the communication device. Once the devices are identified, the judge may request the intervention of communications.

Nevertheless, in cases of terrorism (and other serious crimes), and in the event of emergency, the monitoring can be ordered by the Ministry of Home Affairs or the Secretary of Security. In this event, the fact must be immediately communicated to a judge within 24 hours.

Wiretaps may last a maximum of three months, but may be extended by the judge up to 18 months. Security agents shall inform the judge about the recorded communications and the transcription of the discovered information.

6. Electronic Data Stored by Electronic and Communications Servers' Providers

The new law relates to electronic and communications services providers who are called to cooperate with the judicial police when their collaboration is essential to an investigation, to cross information researches or for gathering intelligence. In any case, communications providers can only be required to give information by means of a court order.

When IP, IMSI or IMEI providers are identified, state agents can apply directly to the providers of telecommunications services or information services, who are required to cooperate.

Spain adopted the Act 15/1999 on information societies and electronic commerce and the Act 25/2007 on retention of data relating to electronic commerce and public communication networks. The latter act implements the European Data Retention Directive 2006/24/CE,[29] that was declared inconsistent with EU law by the European Court of Justice.[30] The Spanish Act imposed an obligation on communication operators to retain certain data generated or processed by them, with the possibility that authorized agents could have access to the data for purposes of preventing and prosecuting serious crimes such as organized crime and terrorism.

Regarding electronic and communication services providers, the Spanish Act on Criminal Procedure, in referring to the crime of terrorism, states in Article 578.4 that "if the facts were committed through services or contents accessible via Internet or using electronic communications services, the court may order the withdrawal of the contents … and to order to the electronic services providers to suppress links pointing to that contents and providers of electronic communications services to prevent access to them or to order to imped access to those illicit contents or services."

Likewise, Article 7 of the new National Security Act states that private entities, when circumstances so require, and always when companies are providers of essential services and critical infrastructure that can affect national security, must collaborate with government. The government must establish the mech-

---

29. Directive 2006/24/EC of the European Parliament and of the Council of 15 March 2006, on the retention of data generated or processed in connection with the provision of electronic communications services for public access or public communications networks.

30. It was declared inconsistent with the privacy principles required by the EU framework. The Courts sentenced that the Directive constituted an interference with the fundamental rights to privacy and protection of personal data (arts.7 and 8 CFREU). The principle of proportionality was not respected. The Directive provisions were not precise enough. (ECJ judgement of April 8, 2014, Case *Digital Rights Ireland Ltd v. Minister for Communications, Marine and Natural Resources and others.* The same position was followed by the Court in its decision of October 6, 2015 about the EU-US Safe Harbour Agreement, in the *Schrems Case.* The Agreement was replaced by a new one, the Shield EU-US Agreement, in 2016.

anisms and forms of collaboration. The question is whether this mechanism creates an open door for forcing communication and Internet providers to collaborate with the government.

On the other hand, the new Act on Citizens' Security also permits access to relevant documentary records for public safety purposes (Article 25.1). This allows the government to exercise control over telephone call centres and thereby over the activities that they perform.

It is still unclear how Spain will implement the recently adopted Directive (EU) 2016/680 of the European Parliament and of the Council of 27 April 2016 on personal data. That data allows competent authorities to access data for the purpose of preventing, investigating, detecting or prosecuting serious criminal offences, and implementation is supposed to occur by 2018.

7. Other Interception of Data and Digital Communications

Other mechanisms for supervising electronic information flow are provided in the new articles contained in the Organic Act on Criminal Procedure. The new Act regulates so-called "undercover agents." These agents, which must be authorized by a judge, may act under assumed identities in electronic conversations through closed channels. Enforcement agents may record pictures or conversations, even at an individual's home, when investigating terrorism. Likewise, the law approves the use of "IT undercover agents," empowered to use computers with a view to exchanging files, entering into chats, even to sending illegal contents, in order to obtain information or discover terrorist plots. This act has been subject to criticism because of the potential risk of abuse: police could incite investigated individuals to commit crimes when acting as "undercover agents." This issue was raised during a Spanish court case against some members of Anonymous, when the defence alleged that the "undercover agent" induced the accused to commit crime.[31]

Police may also confiscate USB devices that they find during home searches. However, a judicial warrant is necessary to gain access to the contents of the device. Exceptionally, in case of emergency, police officers may immediately

31. Carranco, Rebeca: "Un policía infiltrado en Anonymous," *El País*, May 18, 2016.

seize the data and notify a judge at a later time (Article 588 sexies Act on Criminal Procedure).

Similarly, for counter-terrorism investigations, the judge can authorize remote surveillance of personal computers, data bases, USBs or other electronic devices for a month; a period that can be extended for up to three months. The Act establishes requirements regarding the storage of information and data for use in further investigations or as evidence in a trial.

8. Conclusion

Jihadist attacks represent an evident threat to Spain and Europe. We are facing a real global risk. Therefore, the State's involvement is necessary in order to prevent further attacks. The State's response must necessarily include, not only the pursuit of the perpetrators and organizers of the attacks, but also efforts designed to prevent further attacks. How to do this is a challenge, and opinions are divided. What is certain is that any measure that is adopted must conform to the rule of law and be based on respect for human rights. It is essential to understand that citizens' rights are an essential component of the intended security itself.

Fundamental rights are a basic part of a democratic legal system and occupy a privileged position. Such rights should not be infringed except when justified by the general interest in a way that is proportionate to the perceived threat. Consequently, it is imperative to determine which threats to security justify restrictions on human rights and under what conditions. The ECHR warns that there is a risk of overreacting to terrorism: "it is fully aware of the undeniable difficulties of combating terrorism, in particular with regard to obtaining and producing evidence, and of the ravages caused to society by this problem, but considers that such factors cannot justify restricting *to this extent* the rights of the defence of any person charged with a criminal offence."[32] In doing so, the ECHR requires that the nature of the particular threat must be demonstrated and the proportionality of the response be established.

To fight against the risk of further terrorist attacks, cyber-surveillance is a useful and necessary tool. Although technology offers terrorists more and better instruments for the commission of crime, it also assists the government in its efforts at crime prevention. The development of new technical tools, the ex-

32. Case *Hulki Gunes v Turkey*, 19 June 2003, para. 90. See also *case Klass v. Germany*, 6 September 1978.

istence of Internet services providers, which store the data for millions of customers, and more powerful software applications, able to collect and treat data while extracting relevant quality information, create enhanced law enforcement possibilities. In this new scenario, it is necessary to find and respect an appropriate balance between security and privacy.

The use of data, and the oversight of electronic communications, involve mechanisms that the government may utilize in the struggle against terrorism. However, the use of these mechanisms can and must be used with respect for fundamental rights. Spain is on the path toward better regulating the manner in which surveillance takes place. New Spanish legal provisions clarify when a general interest (like protection of national security) justifies invasive police actions. At the same time, the Act establishes the principles that govern cyber-surveillance and the limits that should be imposed on government as a guarantor of fundamental rights.

In Spain, thousands of people, from police officers to politicians to journalists and intellectuals, have lived under the threat of violence by ETA, and tried to respond to the threat of terrorism while respecting the rule of law and fundamental rights (with fatal inaccuracies, of course[33]). Jihadist terror represents a new challenge because of the growth of digitization. However, cyber-surveillance provides a mechanism for fighting against it. Spanish authorities must remember to frame their actions consistently with the rule of law.

Absolute security can never be guaranteed. There will always be a risk of terrorist attacks. Spanish society must do its best to counteract this risk without violating fundamental rights. If we ignore those rights, we will lose the war against terrorism.

---

33. A series of scandals emerged in the past when the practices of undercover policing and surveillance of political parties endangered civil liberties. Remember the creation of the GAL (counter-terrorism groups to fight ETA) Also, Spanish agents' operations were criticized by the United Nations Committee Against Torture in 2002, the UN Special Rapporteur on Torture in 2004, as well as several human rights groups regarding the alleged preexisting severity of various Spain's anti-terrorist operations.

Anne Debet[1]

Cybersurveillance by Law-Enforcement Authorities after the Digital Rights Judgment: Impact on French Law

European Court of Justice (here after ECJ) case law on Data protection was of interest only to a small group of experts and lawyers for a long period of time. As a result, in France, comments on the ECJ's case-law on data protection are scarce. Apart from the judgment declaring invalid the PNR adequacy decision in 2006,[2] and the judgment in the *Scarlet Extended* Case[3] on filtering systems by Internet service providers (ISPs), most French are unaware of the Österreichischer Rundfunk,[4] Bodil Linqvist[5] (one of the most important cases), Huber,[6] Satamedia,[7] Volker et Markus Schecke,[8] and Asnef[9] cases.

Beginning in 2014, the Court's case law on data protection has become the focus of much public attention in France. Virtually everyone is aware of the *Google Spain* case (also known as Costeja)[10] and the *Shrems* case.[11] After years

1. Professor of law, University Paris Descartes

2. Joined Cases C-317/04 and C-318/04, *European Parliament v Council of the European Union*, 30 May 2006.

3. Case C-70/10, *Scarlet Extended SA v Société belge des auteurs, compositeurs et éditeurs SCRL (SABAM)*, 24 November 2011.

4. Joined Cases C-465/00, C-138/01 and C-139/01 *Österreichischer Rundfunk and Others*, 20 may 2003

5. Case C-101/01, *Lindqvist*, 6 November 2003.

6. Case C-524/06 *Huber*, 16 december 2008.

7. Case C-73/07 *Satakunnan Markkinapörssi and Satamedia*, 16 december 2008.

8. Joined Cases C-92/09 and C-93/09 *Volker und Markus Schecke and Eifert*, 9 November 2010.

9. Joined Cases C-468/10 and C-469/10 *ASNEF and FECEMD*, 24 November 2011.

10. Case C-131/12, *Google Spain SL, Google Inc. v Agencia Española de Protección de Datos (AEPD), Mario Costeja González*, 13 May 2014.

11. Case C-362/14, *Maximillian Schrems v Data Protection Commissioner, joined party: Digital Rights Ireland Ltd*, 6 october 2015. See especially on this case: *Küner Chr., Reality and Illusion in EU Data Transfer Regulation Post Schrems, University of Cambridge Faculty of Law Research Paper No. 14/2016.*

of unsuccessful actions by data protection authorities (DPAs) against private as well as public surveillance, the Court has succeeded in fully implementing data protection and privacy rights for individuals. Today, the Court is viewed within the European Union as the primary defender of the citizenry's right to privacy and data protection. While most of the attention has been directed at the Court's actions affecting major Internet actors, like Google and Facebook, the ECJ has also ruled on very important government matters, concerning cybersurveillance by law-enforcement authorities. This contribution will focus on the latter.

The ECJ has become very bold in its interpretation of EU data protection rules.[12] This new approach has become possible due to the consecration of data protection as a fundamental principle of the EU in the Charter of fundamental rights, which became legally binding with the Lisbon Treaty in December 2009. Article 8 of the Charter ("protection of personal data") provides that "1. Everyone has the right to the protection of personal data concerning him or her. 2. Such data must be processed fairly for specified purposes and on the basis of the consent of the person concerned or some other legitimate basis laid down by law. Everyone has the right of access to data which has been collected concerning him or her, and the right to have it rectified. 3. Compliance with these rules shall be subject to control by an independent authority."

Using article 8 and article 7 of the Charter, which lays down the fundamental right to privacy, and is the "twin brother" of article 8 ECHR, the Court was able to invalidate the Data Retention directive with its *Digital Rights* ruling[12] and to declare void the Safe Harbor adequacy decision in the already famous Schrems Case. In its rulings, the Court was forced to deal with large scale surveillance of citizens by law enforcement authorities within the European Union and the United States. Indeed, on both sides of the Atlantic, the commitment to fight terrorism has led governments to restrict the scope of the

12. EU data protection rules are set by Directive 95/46/EC on the protection of individuals with regard to the processing of personal data and on the free movement of such data. This directive will be replaced within two years by the regulation (EU) 2016/679 of 27 April 2016 on the protection of natural persons with regard to the processing of personal data and on the free movement (here after General Regulation on Data Protection or GRDP) and completed by the Directive (EU) 2016/680 of 27 April 2016 on the protection of natural persons with regard to the processing of personal data by competent authorities for the purposes of the prevention, investigation, detection or prosecution of criminal offences or the execution of criminal penalties, and on the free movement of such data, and repealing Council Framework Decision 2008/977/JHA.

13. Joined cases C-293/12 and C-594, *Digital Rights Ireland and Others*, 8 April 2014.

right to privacy in a way that is not compatible with articles 7 and 8 of the Charter.

Recent judgments are therefore very important for the protection of civil liberties. In the first case, the *Digital Rights* judgment, which invalidates the data retention directive, the ECJ provides the foundations for its other rulings. After a quick analysis of this case (I), a study of its—surprising—lack of effects on French law will be the centre of this contribution (II).

I. The ECJ *Digital Rights* Judgment

The ECJ's *Digital Rights* Judgment invalidates the Data Retention Directive. This text needs some explanation in order to enable the reader to fully understand the Court's decision.

The Data Retention Directive

The Data Retention Directive[14] (here after DRD) was adopted in 2006 as a reaction to the 9/11 and to the Madrid (11 mars 2004) and London (7 July 2005) bombings. It was viewed by the EU Member States as a necessary measure in the fight against terrorism. The DRD amended the e-privacy Directive[15] stating notably the fundamental rule regarding the confidentiality of correspondence. Initially, the e-privacy directive left Member States with an option to adopt data retention rules, as a derogation from the confidentiality of communications rule. Member states laws were required to mandate that providers of publically available electronic communications services or of public communications networks—for example Telcos and ISPs (hereafter, 'operators')—retain traffic and location data (excluding content data)[16] for a minimum period of six months up to two years for use in the investigation,

14. Directive 2006/24/EC of the European Parliament and of the Council of 15 March 2006 on the retention of data generated or processed in connection with the provision of publicly available electronic communications services or of public communications networks.

15. Directive 2002/58/EC of 12 July 2002 concerning the processing of personal data and the protection of privacy in the electronic communications sector.

16. The data that needed to be stored are mentioned in article 5 of the directive 2006/24. They are: "the calling and called telephone numbers, the name and address of the subscriber or registered user, the number(s) dialled, the date and time of the log-in and log-off of the Internet access service, data identifying the geographic location of cells"...

detection and prosecution of serious crime. The directive had to be transposed by 2007, but many countries chose not to implement the text in their national laws.

National Reluctances in Transposing the DRD

Many Member States refused to implement the DRD, including. Greece, Sweden, the Netherlands and Austria.[17] In addition, the European Data Protection Supervisor (EDPS) was not particularly keen on the text[18] and even the European Commission voiced criticism.[19]

The Commission has, nevertheless, brought infringement actions against Greece,[20] the Netherlands[21] Sweden[22] and Austria.[23] In other states, national laws transposing the Directive were, sometimes, struck down as violating constitutional rights.[24]

In addition, the Directive was also timely challenged before the ECJ by Ireland. In the 2009 *Ireland v. Council and Parliament* case,[25] the ECJ refused to invalidate the DRD, dismissing Ireland's argument that the DRD had not been adopted on an appropriate legal basis. In the *Digital Rights* case, the ECJ invalidated the Directive, not invalidated on formal grounds, but because of human rights violations.

---

17. See Feiler, L., "The Legality of the Data Retention Directive in Light of the Fundamental Rights to Privacy and Data Protection," European Journal of Law and Technology, Vol. 1, Issue 3, 2010.

18. Opinion of the European Data Protection Supervisor on the Evaluation report from the Commission to the Council and the European Parliament on the Data Retention Directive (Directive 2006/24/EC), https://secure.edps.europa.eu/EDPSWEB/webdav/shared/Documents/Consultation/Opinions/2011/11-05-30_Evaluation_Report_DRD_EN.pdf.

19. European Commission, Evaluation report on the Data Retention Directive (Directive 2006/24/EC), 18 April 2011, COM(2011) 225 final.

20. Case C-211/09, *Commission v. Greece*, 26 November 2009.

21. Case C-192/09, *Commission v. Netherlands*, 9 October, 2009.

22. Case C-185/09, *Commission v. Sweden*, 4 February 2010.

23. Case C-189/09, *Commission v. Austria*, 29 July 2010.

24. See Feiler L., op. cit. and Deshayes B. and Reinhold D., "L'inconstitutionnalité des dispositions allemandes relatives à la conservation des données de connexion—(Cour constitutionnelle allemande du 2 mars 2010)", *Comm. com. Electr.* 2010, Etude 34, also mentioning Bulgaria and Romania. Cf. European Commission, Memo, FAQ The Data Retention Directive, 8 April 2004, p. 2, also referring to the Czech Republic and Cyprus, http://europa.eu/rapid/press-release_MEMO-14-269_en.htm.

25. Case C-301/06, *Ireland v. Council and Parliament*, 10 February 2009.

DRD Invalidation in the *Digital Rights* Case

In this case, the main question submitted by Irish and Austrian courts was whether the DRD was compatible with the right to privacy articulated in Articles 7 and 8 of the Charter. The Court was thus invited to assume jurisdiction over human rights—something that has become more common in recent years[26]—and it has also been asked to undertake proportionality analysis under article 52 of the Charter.[27] On this particular occasion, the ECJ referred to the Charter rather than to the ECHR even though article 8 of the ECHR was mentioned by the national courts. The legal reasoning of the ECJ is, in any event, not really different from the ECtHR's in this particular case as is illustrated by the many references to ECtHR case law.[28]

The Court stated that the DRD involved a wide-ranging and particularly serious interference with the fundamental rights of individuals.[29] This interference had a legal basis, and satisfied an objective of general interest (public security), but it was not proportionate. Moreover, the interference was not precisely circumscribed by provisions ensuring that it was actually limited to what is strictly necessary. The court expressed concern regarding 1) the wide scope of the surveillance—all means of electronic communication, all subscribers and registered users, practically the entire European population with no direct or indirect link with serious crimes, 2) the lack of precision concerning the scope of the access, the procedure to gain access and the way the data could be used, 3) the insufficient precision of the rules concerning the data retention period (6 to 24 months without any distinctions regarding the nature of data).

Furthermore, the Court affirmed that the text did not provide for sufficient safeguards to ensure effective protection of data against the risk of abuse and

---

26. See Fabbrini F., Human Rights in the Digital Age: The European Court of Justice Ruling in the Data Retention Case and its Lessons for Privacy and Surveillance in the United States, Harvard Human Rights Journal . 2015, Vol. 28 Issue 1, p 65–95.

27. See on the relationships between the ECJ and the ECtHR: Roberts A., "Privacy, Data retention and Domination: *Digital Rights Ireland Ltd vs Minister for Communication*", *Modern Law Review 2015, p. 535 et s., spec. p. 539.*

28. See in particular *Digital Rights*, pt 35, 47, 54 and 55.

29. In its Memo (European Commission, Memo, FAQ The Data Retention Directive, 8 april 2004, http://europa.eu/rapid/press-release_MEMO-14-269_en.htm), the Commission states that *"based on figures provided by 17 Member States, there were about 1.56 million requests for data in 2008 and, based on statistics from 12 Member States, there were about 2.66 million requests in 2012. The most frequently requested type of data overall concerns mobile telephony"* (p. 2).

against any unlawful access and use of that data (insufficient security requirements and possible transfers of this data outside the EU).

The decision can be seen as the beginning of a new line of ECJ case law, strongly defending an individual's rights to privacy. *Google Spain* and *Schrems* follow naturally from the *Digital rights* judgment.[30] Regarding the effects of this judgment on National Laws, the European Commission in a document titled "Memo of Frequently Asked Questions," issued immediately after the Digital Rights Case, states that "*National legislation needs to be amended only with regard to aspects that become contrary to EU law after a judgment by the European Court of Justice. Furthermore, a finding of invalidity of the Directive does not cancel the ability for Member States under the e-Privacy Directive (2002/58/EC) to oblige retention of data.*" For its part, the article 29 WP urged Member states to evaluate the consequences of the Digital Rights Judgment on national data retention laws.[31] Those different statements have led to many uncertainties concerning national laws. A study of French law provides a pertinent illustration of this fact.

II. Effect of *Digital Rights* Judgment on French Law

Impact of the *Digital Rights* Judgment on National Laws

The impact of the *Digital Rights* Judgment on national law is still uncertain.[32] The Court only invalidated the Data Retention Directive. National laws implementing the directive are still legally binding and some of these laws were adopted before the Directive. Article 15 of the ePrivacy Directive allows Member States to establish a data retention system to the extent that those systems are compatible with the data protection and privacy rights established by the

---

30. Some other earlier judgments also showed that the Court was really invested in defending data protection rights like the PNR case (Joined Cases C-317/04 and C-318/04, *European Parliament v Council of the European Union*, 30 May 2006), but they were less spectacular than the annulment of a Directive. Furthermore, in the PNR Case, the invalidation of the adequacy decision was founded on a formal argument (lack of competence of the Commission) and not on the violation of fundamental rights.

31. 29 WP, Statement on the ruling of the Court of Justice of the European Union (CJEU) which invalidates the Data Retention Directive, WP 220, 1 August 2014.

32. See WP 29 analysis, in its Working Document on surveillance of electronic communications for intelligence and national security purposes, adopted on 5 December 2014, WP 228, p. 37.

Charter as interpreted by the ECJ.[33] As shown in the 2016 report of the European Union Agency for fundamental rights (FRA), many Judges and legislators of EU countries have decided to modify national data retention rules.[34]

Constitutional courts of Belgium, Bulgaria, Poland and Slovakia decided in 2015 that their countries' data retention regimes were unconstitutional.[35] In Netherlands, the District Court of The Hague concluded that Dutch law violated the right to privacy. In the United Kingdom, the High Court of Justice ruled, on 17 July 2015, in the *Davis/Watson* case,[36] that certain sections of the Data Retention and Investigatory Powers Act of 2014 (DRIPA) were not compatible with the right to the respect of private life and communications, and to the protection of personal data. An appeal was filed against this decision.[37] Some cases are also pending in Hungary and Sweden.

The conclusions that can be drawn from the invalidation of these data retention regimes vary. In Austria, for example the Supreme Court—which revoked the national law implementing the Data Retention Directive—concluded that the operator must grant access to law enforcement agencies of location data retained for billing purposes.

Reforms of applicable data retention regimes have been undertaken in some Member States—spontaneously in Croatia, Denmark, Estonia, Finland,

---

33. National laws must be compatible with the Charter in so far that they fall within the scope of EU law. It might be argued founded on article 15 of the eprivacy directive that is truly the case (see on this matter: 29, WP, WP 220, cited above, spec. p. 2 and Conseil d'Etat, *Digital World and fundamental rights, Le Numérique et les droits fondamentaux*, Etude annuelle 2014, La documentation française, 2014, p.199–200). The mere existence of the Directive (EU) 2016/680 of the European Parliament and of the Council of 27 April 2016 on the protection of natural persons with regard to the processing of personal data by competent authorities for the purposes of the prevention, investigation, detection or prosecution of criminal offences or the execution of criminal penalties tends to confirm this position.

34. European Union Agency for fundamental rights (FRA), Fundamental Rights Report for 2016, http://fra.europa.eu/sites/default/files/fra_uploads/fra-2016-fundamental-rights-report-2016-0_en.pdf, p. 124.

35. This presentation of National reactions after the Digital Rights judgment is a summary of the one found in the Fundamental Rights Report cited above.

36. High Court of justice, Queen's Bench Division, Divisional Court, David Davis MP, Tom Watson MP, Peter Brice, Geoffrey Lewis v. Secretary of State for the Home Department, Case No: CO/3665/2014, CO/3667/2014, CO/3794/201, 17 july 2015, https://www.judiciary.gov.uk/wp-content/uploads/2015/07/davis_judgment.pdf, [2015] EWHC 2092 (Admin).

37. *Cf. infra.*

Lithuania and after the Constitutional courts' rulings in Poland, Belgium and Slovakia.

Impact of the Digital Rights Judgment on French Law

France is not mentioned at all by the FRA report 2016 on Fundamental rights. Indeed, unlike other member states, there was not much reaction in France to the *Digital Rights* judgement, or following the Paris terrorists attacks of January 2015 and November 2015. After the attacks, the French government opted to strengthen its means of surveillance regime rather than to reconsider it from a human rights protection perspective.

The French data retention regime is not based upon the Data Retention Directive. This perhaps explains why French public authorities do not seem very concerned by the ECJ judgment. The French regime is very complex because it does not provide for unified rules governing data retention and access, but rather articulates the governing rules in different laws and codes.

Regarding the obligation to retain data, the legislative framework is long-established and results from the combination of two texts. On the one hand, article L. 34-1 of the Posts and Electronic Communications Code (Codes des postes et des communications électroniques, here after CPCE) derogates the requirement to anonymize data and requires operators to retain data for a period of one year. This obligation was established in the Law of 15 November 2001 on everyday security.[38] Regulatory provisions (art. R. 10-12 to R. 10-22 CPCE) completed this regime. On the other hand, article 6 of the law n° 2004-575 of 21 June 2004 on confidence in the digital economy requires Internet service providers and Internet hosting companies to hold and retain identification data of any person who contributed to the creation of online content. A decree, long-expected and finally published in 2011,[39] lists the data which must be retained by the ISPs and hosting companies for a period of one year.

Rules governing access to data by law enforcement authorities are articulated in the Homeland Security Code (Code de la sécurité Intérieure, here after

---

38. Law n° 2001-1062 of 15 November 2001 on Everyday Security, article 29.

39. Decree n° 2011-219 of 25 February 2011 on the retention and communication of data allowing for the identification of any person having contributed to the creation of online content. The decree was challenged before the administrative jurisdiction. Arguments about privacy rights were not examined by the French Council of State which declared the text valid (Conseil d'État, 20 novembre 2013, n° 347349, *Communication commerce électronique* 2014, comm. n° 9, obs. A lepage).

CSI). Applicable rules have evolved over time. It the beginning, access to data was only permitted through the framework of judicial procedures. Then administrative access to the data was granted in an effort to prevent acts of terrorism, in 2006,[40] and progressively for other purposes. These various purposes are now mentioned in Article L. 811-3 of the CSI. Procedure which has been significantly amended by the law of 18 December 2013 on military programming[41] and more recently by the Law on Intelligence[42] that reorganizes the entire regime in articles L. 851-1 and following articles of the CSI, which will soon come into force. The legislative objectives of these laws was to establish a general and unified legal framework for intelligence activities, even though French Intelligence services have other means, provided by this law, to access traffic data (use of IMSI catchers for example).

Regarding the ECJ's denunciation in the Digital Rights judgment regarding the weaknesses of guaranties, French law allows the retention of metadata concerning any person and not just those who have a link with serious crime. Therefore, the interference with private life must be considered as very wide and serious. The list of purposes justifying access to data is particularly long: article 811-3 CSI containing 7 items, one of which has 3 subdivisions and strict rules set up purpose limitations (article L 822-3, CSI). It is difficult to say whether this list is too broad or whether French law is sufficiently precise, since the purposes are defined and limited. Since the 2015 law on intelligence, the access regime to traffic data has been clearly framed by articles L. 821-1 and following of the CSI. The authorization of the Prime Minister, after consultation with an administrative authority[43] (Commission nationale de contrôle des techniques de renseignements), with few exceptions narrowly defined,[44] is needed in order to access data. Logs and data use controls must be implemented pursuit to the new texts (art. 822-1 and following, CSI) and there is a possibility to submit a claim to the French Council of State (article L. 311-4-1 of the administrative justice Code).

A thorough study of French law should be undertaken to see if there are any incompatibilities with the requirements established by the ECJ in the Digital Rights Judgment. In fact, as surprising as it may seem, very few per-

40. Law n° 2006-64 of 23 January 2006 on the fight against terrorism and containing various provisions relating to security and border controls, article 6.

41. Law n° 2013-1168 of 18 December 2013 on the military programming for the years 2014 to 2019 and containing various provisions regarding defense and national security, article 20.

42. Law n° 2015-912 of 24 July 2015 on Intelligence.

43. Article L. 821-1 CSI and following articles.

44. Article L. 821-5 CSI, for example.

sons or institutions in France have thought about this issue. Three institutions recently invoked the *Digital Rights* Judgment regarding French law: the Council of State in its 2014 report on Digital world and fundamental Rights,[45] the French Data Protection Authority (CNIL) in its opinion on regulation adopted in order to enforce the law on military programming[46] and the Rights' Defender (Défenseur des droits) in its opinion about the Law on Intelligence.[47]

However, there has been no discussion of this issue by the Constitutional Council in its official comments—published on its website—concerning its decision n° 2015-713 DC about the law on Intelligence[48] and concerning its decision n° 2015-478 QPC on a priority preliminary ruling on the issue of constitutionality (QPC) concerning some articles of the law on military programming.[49] It must be said that the Constitutional council does not often refer to other jurisdictions protecting Human rights in its comments. Sometimes, though, it makes references to the position of the European Court of Human rights. The ECJ's case law seems to be quite completely forgotten by the French constitutional judges not only for the state cybersurveillance matters, but also elsewhere. It is probably a sign, among many, of a lack of openness of this jurisdiction, diverging widely from the other member States' constitutional courts.

The Council of state, although apparently interested by the subject in its 2014 report,[50] is nevertheless completely mute about the *Digital Rights* Judg-

45. Conseil d'Etat, *Digital World and fundamental rights, Le Numérique et les droits fondamentaux*, Etude annuelle 2014, La documentation française, 2014, p.199–201. The Council of State does not give a clear answer on whether it should be necessary to change some aspects of French law in regards with the Digital rights judgment.

46. CNIL, Delibération n° 2014-484 of the 4 December 2014 setting up an opinion on the project of Decree concerning administrative access to traffic data and implementing article 246-2 of the Homeland Security Code (Délibération n° 2014-484 du 4 décembre 2014 portant avis sur un projet de décret relatif à l'accès administratif aux données de connexion et portant application de l'article L. 246-4 du code de la sécurité intérieure).

47. Rights' Defender (Défenseur des droits), Opinion n° 15-04, 2 April 2015. It needs to be noted that the French Data Protection Authority (CNIL) did not mention the Digital Rights Judgments in its opinion on this law (Deliberation n° 2015-078 of 5 march 2015 commenting on the Law project on Intelligence).

48. Decision n° 2015-713 DC of 23 july 2015 concerning the Law on Intelligence and the "*Cahiers du Conseil constitutionnel*" ("Commentaire" Link on the webpage publishing the decision).

49. Decision n° 2015-478 QPC of 24 july 2015, Association French Data Network and others [administrative access to traffic data] and the "cahiers du Conseil" ("Commentaire" Link, on the webpage publishing the decision).

50. See previous references.

ment in 2016,[51] when it was asked to review the decree implementing the law on military programming in light of the rights enshrined in the European Convention on Human rights and also in light of articles 7 and 8 of the Charter on fundamental rights. The Council of state considered the text valid because it was detailed regarding data that could be accessed, agents and services who could access the data, the maximum length of data retention by law enforcement authorities, and imposed strict procedures and means of control. The Council therefore considered that this interference affects the rights guaranteed by the ECHR in a proportionate manner and that similar conclusions should be reached regarding article 7 and 8 of the Charter. The *Digital Rights* Judgment was not even mentioned even though the Council of state is generally not as reluctant as the Constitutional Council to refer to the ECJ's case law.

Precisions to Be Given at European Level

The differences between Member States regarding their responses to the *Digital Rights* Judgment surely needs to be examined at a European level. The first precision might be given by the ECJ itself. Indeed, an English Court of Appeal in the *Davis/Watson* case[52] requested a preliminary ruling from the CJEU as to the effect of the *Digital Rights* case.[53] Two questions were raised by the British courts. First, the ECJ is being asked whether its judgment in Digital Rights imposes mandatory EU requirements as applied to a Member State's domestic regime governing access to data retained in accordance with national legislation, and whether it complies with Articles 7 and 8 of the EU Charter. Then, more generally, the ECJ is requested to clarify whether its *Digital Rights Ireland* judgment expanded the scope of Articles 7 and/or 8 of the EU Charter beyond those articulated in Article 8 of the European Convention of Human

51. Council of State, 12 février 2016, n° 3881134.

52. Court of Appeal (England & Wales) (Civil Division), Secretary of State for the Home Department v David Davis, Tom Watson, Peter Brice, Geoffrey Lewis, Case C1/ 2015 /2612, 20 November 2015, https://www.judiciary.gov.uk/wp-content/uploads/2015/11 /davis_final.pdf, [2015] EWCA Civ 1185.

53. Reference for a preliminary ruling from Court of Appeal (England & Wales) (Civil Division) made on 28 December 2015—Secretary of State for the Home Department v David Davis, Tom Watson, Peter Brice, Geoffrey Lewis (Case C-698/15) and Order of the President of the Court deciding that the case shall be determined pursuant to the expedited procedure provided for in Article 105(1) of the Rules of Procedure of the Court. See for a question about Swedish law: Request for a preliminary ruling from the Kammarrätten i Stockholm (Sweden) lodged on 4 May 2015—Tele2 Sverige AB v Post-och telestyrelsen, (Case C-203/15).

Rights ("ECHR") as established in the jurisprudence of the European Court of Human Rights ("ECtHR").

The answer given by the European Court might not be sufficient. Most EU countries view their data retention regimes as necessary measures that are needed to fight serious crimes, including terrorism. In the meeting of the Justice and Home Affairs Council, held the 3rd and 4rth of December 2015, a majority of country delegations therefore invited the Commission to present a new legislative initiative designed to provide a legal framework for data retention across the EU, as soon as possible.[54] The consequences of the ruling of the Court almost two years after are still unknown.

Conclusion: Two conclusions can be drawn from this short presentation on the effects of the *Digital Rights* Judgment. An analysis of this case law reveals the major role played by the ECJ regarding data protection. The Court, through its bold interpretation of the Charter, has taken part in the reconstruction of the law, with the side effects that are always evident in case law, including: uncertainties regarding its real scope and its general lack of clarity. The study also demonstrates the particular deafness of French authorities in terms of taking into account the major role now played by the ECJ on human rights matters. The former President of the Constitutional Council underlined the importance of the convergence of constitutional and conventional control.[55] Let us hope that in the future, the council will also realize the place that should be given to ECJ case law!

---

53. Council of the European Union (2015), 'Outcome of the Council meeting', Press release, 3 and 4 December 2015, http://www.consilium.europa.eu/en/meetings/jha/2015/12/03-04/.

54. J.-L Debré, Speech for the fifth anniversary of the priority preliminary ruling on the issue of constitutionality (QPC) , 2 march 2015.

Olivia Tambou[1]

Profiling in the General Data Protection Regulation: Progress, But More Improvements Are Needed[2]

Recently, the European Data Protection Authorities (hereinafter DPAs) revealed how Facebook massively tracks Internet users, including those who do not have a Facebook account. It was clearly demonstrated that the website analyses the Internet users' behaviours from an advertising-based point of view without properly informing them and getting their consent.[3] After Edward Snowden's disclosures about government surveillance programs and the Facebook cases,[4] it is hard to believe that most people are not aware of the fact that public authorities as well as private companies collect their personal data in order to analyse their behaviour.

Paradoxically, most people are merely unaware of this multi-level surveillance, but share at the same time the feeling that there is nothing they can do about it. Many people assume that being profiled is the normal counterpart of their security or of accessing free or personalised services or goods. Some of us do not see it as a real danger because we think that we have nothing to hide. Those who are more eager to protect their personal data are sometimes demobilised. It seems too complicated, and time-consuming to design concrete and

---

1. Associate Professor at University Paris-Dauphine, PSL Research University Introduction

2. This paper has been prepared for the Cyber Surveillance forum which was held at Université Paris-Dauphine, France, on June 15th–16th 2016. I will very much welcome and value comments, critiques, suggested readings you consider relevant: olivia.tambou@dauphine.fr.

3. See the CNIL decision n° 2016–007 of January 27, issuing formal notice to Facebook Inc. and Facebook Ireland, and my comments La CNIL donne une leçon de droit européen à notre ami américain Facebook, Dalloz Actualité, Le droit en débats, 23 février 2016

4. ECJ 6 october 2015, Schrems case C-362/14 see my Tribune, Propos libres autour de l'invalisation par la CJUE de la decision Safe Harbor, Dalloz droit en débats, 9 October 2015.

individual solutions. It is most of the time an "all-or-nothing" solution. So, for most people it is hard to conceive of how to benefit from the good part of the profiling without losing control over their personal data and being manipulated or discriminated against.

The concept of profiling in the digital age has been the subject of major studies for the last decade.[5] In this context, Mireille Hildebrandt said, profiling refers "to a set of technologies, which share at least one common characteristic: the use of algorithms or other techniques to create, discover or construct knowledge from huge sets of data." The benefit and concerns about profiling have risen with the development of the information society. This should be supported by Big Data, combined with the development of the storage capacity of Cloud Computing and the smart technologies. The concept of Big Data is usually described as the "3Vs": volume, variety and velocity. It shows that the volume of the collected and processed data, the variety of sources and formats[6] as well as the capacity to analyse them in real time, are unprecedented. 'Big Data' refers to novel ways in which organizations, including government and businesses, combine diverse digital datasets and then use statistics and other data mining techniques to extract from them both hidden information and surprising correlations.[7] In other words, Big Data offers au-

5. Hildebrandt, Mireille, Gutwirth, Serge (Eds.), Profiling the European Citizen, Springer 2008; Francesca Bosco, Niklas Creemers, Valeria Ferraris, Daniel Guagnin, and Bert-Jaap Koops, Profiling Technologies and Fundamental Rights and Values: Regulatory Challenges and Perspectives from European Data Protection Authorities; Georgia Skouma and Laura Léonard On-line Behavioral Tracking: What May Change After the Legal Reform on Personal both in Data Protection in Serge Gutwirth Ronald Leenes Paul de Hert Editor, Reforming European Data protection law, springer, 2015; Alain Grosjean, Le profilage: un défi pour la protection des données à caractère personnel, in Les enjeux européens et mondiaux de la protection des données personnelles, sous la direction d'Alain Grosjean, Larcier, 2015, p. 277; Eskens, Sarah Johanna, Profiling the European Citizen in the Internet of Things: How Will the General Data Protection Regulation Apply to this Form of Personal Data Processing, and How Should It? (February 29, 2016). Available at SSRN: http://ssrn.com/abstract=2752010; Profiling project: Profiling: protecting citizens' rights fighting illicit profiling, Final report 2015. Spiecker genannt Döhmann, I., Tambou, O., Bernal, P., Hu, M., Molinaro, C., Negre, E., Wolfgang Sarlet, I., Schertel Mendes, L., Witzleb, N., & Yger, F., Multi-Country The Regulation of Commercial Profiling — A Comparative Analysis *European Data Protection Law* Review Volume 2, Issue 4 (2016) pp. 535–554.

6. Like sensors, cameras, geospatial technologies, mobile applications, website, wearable, devices monitoring physical activity like the Apple watch, the Fitbit. An important volume of data is shared by the individuals themselves though mobile apps or social networks.

7. Ira S. Rubinstein, Big Data: The End of Privacy or a New Beginning?, International Data Privacy Law 2013 p.1

tomated-decisions based on the classification and the evaluation of human behaviours. Antoinette Rouvroy describes this phenomenon as "algorithmic governability." In this context, the ethics of Big Data have recently raised some concerns.[8] The main concern is how to avoid decisions of excluding or losing opportunities based on false predictions about individuals. Margaret Hu has illustrated the development in the U.S. of the "Big Data blacklisting" phenomenon through government-led Big Data.[9] She considered that "Big Data blacklisting" is the process of categorizing individuals as administratively "guilty until proven innocent" by virtue of suspicious digital data and database screening results."

The word "profiling" was introduced in the European law by the General Data Protection Regulation (herein after GDPR) adopted on the 26th of April 2016.[10] The GDPR repealed the Directive 95/46 and will apply as from May 25th, 2018. This paper discusses the real progress of the proposed European legal framework of profiling. It falls into two main sections. The first part evaluates the progress of the proposed regulation of profiling in the GDPR. It presents the element of the harmonised definition of profiling in the EU Law, as well as the new guaranties of the regulation of profiling. The second part discusses the need for improvements. It demonstrates the need for a more consistent and comprehensive approach of profiling based on the reality of Big Data and smart technologies. It argues that the effectiveness of the data subject will depend on the reality of the implementation of the data controller accountability principle and the coordination of the regulation through DPAs. It considers that the legal framework of profiling in the GDPR has to be completed with guaranties that should be introduced in European texts currently under discussion, such as the e-privacy Directive and the trade secrets directive. Special attention to this issue in the European regulation on the online platform should also be given. Before going further, a

8. Richards, Neil M. and King, Jonathan H., Big Data Ethics (May 19, 2014). Wake Forest Law Review, 2014. Available at SSRN: http://ssrn.com/abstract=2384174; See European Data protection supervisor, Opinion 4/2015 Towards a new digital Ethics, data dignity and technology, adopted on 11 September 2015. Since January 2016 the EDPS have established an Ethics advisory Group. This concern include the professional see the public consultation open by the Publicité et Big Data, from the Conseil de l'éthique publicitaire de l'autorité de regulation professionnelle de la publicité on April 2016.

9. Margaret Hu, Big Data Blacklisting, Florida Law review 2015, 1735.

10. EU regulation 2016/679 of the European parliament and of the council of 27 April 2016, on the protection of natural persons with regard to the processing of personal data and on the free movement of such data, OJEU L 119/1 from the 4 May 2016.

general overview of the reform of the European data protection must be provided for.

a) The Context and the New Legal Basis of the GDPR

The European personal data protection is based on the Data Protection Directive 95/46 EC. In 2012, the European Commission adopted a reform package with two proposals—the GDPR, and the Directive on the protection of individuals with regard to the processing of personal data by competent authorities for the purposes of prevention, investigation, detection or prosecution of criminal offences or the execution of criminal penalties, and the free movement of such data. This package was designed as a comprehensive reform of the EU legal framework that must be linked with "the second wave of global privacy law,"[11] as the OECD Reform and the U.S. reform are called. These new rules aim at facing the three challenges encountered by the evolution of technologies, in particular the surge of Big Data and analytics, the importance of the digital economy that demands creating trust in the on-line environment and globalisation. The GDPR is a monster text of 99 articles, whereas the current Directive 95/46 has only 34 articles. The GDPR is based on the new Article 16 of the Treaty on the Functioning of the European Union (TFEU), introduced by the Treaty of Lisbon. This Article anchors personal data protection in the fundamental rights.[12] It creates an autonomous right of data protection derived from the right of privacy.[13] This global and human rights perspective of the European data protection is considered as one of the main differences

11. Omer Tene, Reforming data protection in Europe and beyond: a critical assessment of the second wave of global privacy laws, in Artemio Vicente Rallo Lombarte, María del Rosario García Mahamut. Hacia un Nuevo Derecho Europeo de Protección de Datos. 2015 Valencia, Tirant Lo Blanch, p. 142.

12. Gloria González Fuster, The Emergence of Personal Data Protection as a Fundamental Right of the EU, Springer 2014.

13. For more details, see Julian Kokott and Christop Sobotta, "The distinction between privacy and data protection in the jurisprudence of the CJEU and the ECtHR, International Data Privacy Law," vol.3, ed.4, 2013, 222–228. For a good synthesis about the concept of privacy see Rachel L Finn, David Wright and Michael Friedewald, Seven Types of Privacy, in Serge Gutwirth, Ronald Leenes, Paul de Hert, Yves Poullet Editors, European Data Protection: Coming of Age, Springer 2013, p. 3–32.

with the U.S. approach.[14] The U.S. does not have a "dedicated data protection law, but instead regulates primarily by industry, on a sector-by-sector basis."[15]

Whereas the GDPR benefits from Article 16 TFEU, it is also considered to be a masterpiece of the digital single market.[16] In other words, as the proposal of the EU Commission clearly claims it to be, the GDPR has the double ambition "to ensure consistent and high level of protection of individuals and to remove the obstacles to flows of personal data."

b) The Integrated Vision of European Data Protection Law

In order to understand the EU Data protection Reform, here are some explanations about the integrated vision of data protection law. Many scholars[17] have demonstrated that the right of individual control or informational self-determination is becoming a "meta-principle" of the European data protection law. This vision is also shared by the European national authorities.[18] This rights-

---

14. Constance Chevallier-Goyers, "Personal data protection: confrontation between the European Union and the United States of America, in The European Union and the United States, processes, policies and projects, sous la direction." Yann Echinard, Albane Geslin, Michel Gueldry, Fabien Terpan, Larcier 2013; For an analysis of the convergence of the US and European approach see C. Levallois-Barth, "Legal Challenges Facing Global Privacy Governance," in cahier de prospective, The futures of Privacy, Editor Carine Dartiguepeyrou, Fondation Télécom, Institut Mines-Télécom, February 2014, p. 55, http://cvpip.wp.mines-telecom.fr/files/2014/02/14-02-The-futur-of-privacy-cahier-de-prospective.pdf; David Vladeck, Separated by common goals: A U.S. Perspective on narrowing the U.S.-EU privacy divide, in Hacia un Nuevo Derecho Europeo de Protección de Datos op.cit. p. 207–243.

15. Lise L. Sotto and Aaron P. Simpson, United States, in Data protection and Privacy in 26 jurisdictions worldwide, contributing editor Rosemary P. Jay, Published by Getting Deal Through, 2014 p. 191, https://www.huntonprivacyblog.com/files/2011/04/DDP2015_United_States.pdf; United States, Kurt Wimmer in Data protection and privacy, Jurisdictional comparisons, general Editor Monika Kuschenwsky, Covington and Burling LLP, European Lawyer reference, pp.885–909.

16. "A Digital Single Market Strategy for Europe," Com (2015) 192 final 6th May 2015 http://ec.europa.eu/priorities/digital-single-market/docs/dsm-communication_en.pdf

17. Antoinette Rouvroy and Yves Poullet, 'The Right to Informational Self-Determination and the Value of Self Development: Reassessing the Importance of Privacy for Democracy' in Serge Gutwirth and others (eds), Reinventing Data Protection (Springer, Dordrecht; Heidleberg; London; New York 2009).

18. See the Census decision of the Constitutionnal Court of Germany 65 BVerfGE 1 (1983), French Conseil d'Etat, Étude annuelle 2014—Le numérique et les droits fonda-

based approach is implemented in the European data protection law by giving the data subject certain subjective rights at the core of the profiling regime. The principle of the consent of the data subject, the principle of transparency of the processing, in particular the right to be informed, the right to access, rectification and erasure, and the right of restriction of processing all are part of this context. The GDPR intends to improve the rights introduced by the EC Directive 95/46. The new right of data portability[19] and the right to be forgotten are also a good illustration of this vision of individual control over personal data.

The second vision is a risk-based regulation approach.[20] This notion entails at least gathering knowledge about harms and taking measures to control those dangers.[21] Some provisions of the EC Directive refer to a risk-based approach, including the security obligation (Article 17), the prior checking in order "to present specific risks to the rights and freedoms of data subjects," (Article 20), the legal regime applicable to processing of sensitive data (Article 8). In the GDPR, genetic data and biometric data are acknowledged as sensitive data requiring extra protection.

During the discussions of the GDPR, there were two conflicting approaches to the regulation of risks.[22] The first one has been presented as "an alternative to the well-established data protection right and principles."[23] In other words, it has been advocated that the respect of the data protection law should be fo-

mentaux, La Documentation française, Paris 2014, p. 264 which emphasises that "data protection law is a right of informational self-determination" and reject the property vision of data protection law and also the French Digital Republic Act project which concretises this right by the right of self-housing digital data (article 20 droit d'auto-heberger ses données), right to determinate and control the use of personal data (article 26), the right to data portability (article 21), more individual sovereignty on the social networks for the minor and the decease person.

19. Eva Fialová, "Data portability and informational self-determination," Masaryk Univerisity Journal of law and technology, 2014, p. 45; Zanfir, Gabriela, The Right to Data Portability in the Context of the EU Data Protection Reform (March 12, 2012), International Data Privacy Law, Vol. 2, No. 3, 2012.

20. Centre for Information Policy Leadership, the A Risk-based Approach to Privacy: Improving Effectiveness in Practice, 19 June 2014 https://www.hunton.com/files/upload/Post-Paris_Risk_Paper_June_2014.pdf.

21. See Raphaël Gellert, "Data protection: a risk regulation? Between the risk management of everything and the precautionary alternative," International Data privacy Law 2015, Vol.5 p. 3 Antti Antikainen, Risk-Based Approach as a Solution to Secondary Use of Personal Data, master's thesis of the University of Helsinki, 2014.

22. See Statement of the WP29 on the role of a risk-based approach in data protection legal frameworks, adopted on 30 May 2014.

23. Ibid. p. 2.

cused only on the processing of data with high-risk. The concerns expressed in particular by the DPAs and NGO's seem to have paved the way for a second conception. This other vision of the risk-based regulation approach is more of a "scalable and proportionate approach to compliance."[24] The promotion of privacy-by-design and privacy-by-default principles and the certification for instance, are means to ensure that a risk-based approach can tame the privacy harm due to technologies. The introduction of the principle of accountability in the GDPR is also an illustration of this risk-based regulation approach. According to the definition adopted by the European Data Protection Supervisor (EDPS), the principle of accountability is to "ensure that data controllers are more generally in control and in position to ensure and demonstrate compliance with data protection principles in practice."[25] The data controllers will not be obliged to first declare their processing as counterparts any more. However, the data controller shall endorse a prior data privacy impact assessment when a processing "is likely to result in high-risks to the rights and freedoms of national persons."[26]

The third vision of the data protection law is based on fair processing obligations.[27] It relies on fundamental principles applicable to the controllers, such as legitimacy, data minimisation, purpose limitation, transparency, data integrity, data accuracy, data quality,[28] and a special care for sensitive data, among others. The data breach notification[29] obligation to the supervisory authority and the communication of the personal data breach to the data subject introduced in the GDPR illustrate this vision.[30]

---

24. Ibid.

25. Peter Hustinx, "The Strategic Context and the Role of Data Protection Authorities in the Debate on the Future of Privacy", European Privacy and Data Protection Commissioners' Conference Prague, Czech Republic, 29 April 2010, https://secure.edps.europa.eu/EDPSWEB/webdav/shared/Documents/EDPS/Publications/Speeches/2010/10-04-29_Speech_Future_Privacy_EN.pdf

26. Article 35 GDPR.

27. See Bart van der Sloot, Do data protection rules protect the individual and should they? An assessment of the proposed General Data Protection Regulation International Data Privacy Law 2014 p. 307, p. 310.

28. See article 5.

29. Carlos Alberto Saiz Peña, La notificación de brechas de seguridad, in Hacia un Nuevo Derecho Europeo de Datos, op. cit. p. 77.1

30. The GDPR introduces a general data breach notification requirement that will apply across all industry sectors and will require data controllers to notify the competent supervisory authority within 72 hours after becoming aware of a data breach, unless they can provide a reasoned justification for the delay.

This paper will demonstrate how these three visions of the European data protection law are integrated in the new legal framework of the profiling.

§ 1 The Elements of Progress

Before the adoption of the GDPR, the Council of Europe had provided the unique European definition of profiling. The masterpiece of this international organisation created in 1949 is the well-known Convention for the Protection of Human Rights (herein after, ECHR). The ECHR includes in Article 8 the right of privacy as a fundamental right. Furthermore, it develops a more specific legal protection under the Convention for the Protection of Individuals with regard to Automatic Processing of Personal Data known as "Convention No. 108." To date, this Convention No. 108 has been ratified by the 47 member states of the Council of Europe and Uruguay, Mauritius and Senegal.[31] Whereas Convention No. 108 is a binding legal instrument with a universal scope, the definition of profiling proposed by the Council of Europe being only referred to in a recommendation dated back to 2010.[32] Thus, the first added value of the GDPR is to provide the first harmonised compulsory definition of profiling in EU Law.

A. The first European Harmonised Compulsory Definition of Profiling in the EU

The GDPR provides the first harmonised compulsory definition of the notion of profiling that will be directly applicable in the 28 EU member states. "Profiling means any form of automated processing of personal data consisting of the use of personal data to evaluate certain personal aspects relating to a natural person, in particular to analyse or predict aspects concerning that natural person's performance at work, economic situation, health, personal preferences, interests, reliability, behaviour, location or movements."[33]

This definition is based on three main elements. First, profiling needs an automated processing of personal data. The concept of automated processing

---

31. See the Chart of signatures and ratifications of Treaty 108. http://www.coe.int/en/web/conventions/full-list/-/conventions/treaty/108/signatures

32. The protection of individuals with regard to automatic processing of personal data in the context of profiling Recommendation CM/Rec(2010)13 and explanatory memorandum.

33. See article 4 §4 GDPR. This harmonised definition has been introduced by the European Parliament in March 2014.

has not been harmonised yet.[34] It should include all processing based on a computer, a camera, a smartphone, or a machine to machine process. The GDPR definition of personal data is very similar to the current wording of the 95/46 EC Directive and still based on a comprehensive approach of identifiability. "Personal data means any information relating to an identified or identifiable natural data subject; an identifiable natural person is one who can be identified, directly or indirectly, in particular by reference to an identifier such as a name, an identification number, location data, an online identifier or to one or more factors specific to the physical, physiological, genetic, mental, economic, cultural or social identity of that natural person."[35] This broad definition embraces the nominative identity (names but also genetic and biometric features etc.) and the virtual or digital identity of the person, such as any pseudonym, avatar, logging code, cookies, IP addresses, etc.[36]

After long discussions, the pseudonymous data has not been introduced as a new category of personal data with a lighter regime. This proposal has been seen as a Trojan horse allowing the actors of the digital economy to dangerously develop profiling. The GDPR refers much more to "pseudonymisation" as a data security measure[37] aiming at making it harder to identify a natural person. This illustrates the above-mentioned conflicting visions of the risk-based approach of the European Data protection law.

Secondly, this definition put forward a purposive approach of profiling illustrated by two types of objectives—analysing and predicting the behaviour of the natural person.

Thirdly, by listing them, the definition embodies the objects to which this purposive approach could apply. Evaluating the performance at work refers to the video or electronic surveillance of employees for instance. An identification number could be one such as social security and taxpayers identifiers. The location data refers to all the techniques based on GPS or sensors, like

34. Article 4 only defines the concept of processing.

35. One of the main differences with the definition of the wording of the EC95/46 Directive is the addition of concrete examples of identifiers such as "name", "location data, "online identifier" and the term of "genetic identity".

36. This classification is based on the approach of Anne Debet, Jean Massot, Nathalie Metallinos, Informatique et libertés, la protection à caractère données personnelles en droit français et européen, Lextenso 2015 p. 248.

37. See Zuiderveen Borgesius, Frederik J., Singling Out People Without Knowing Their Names—Behavioural Targeting, Pseudonymous Data, and the New Data Protection Regulation (February 16, 2016). Available at SSRN: http://ssrn.com/abstract=2733115 p. 26–30.

RFID tags, or public WIFI, that allow your smartphone or mobile application to show exactly where you are. Location data are at the core of the Internet of Things and the system of public-transport innovations in the smart cities.

B. The Guaranties of the European Legal Framework Relating to Profiling

1. *The Novelties of the Article 22 GDPR*

New guaranties have been introduced in Article 22, which now deals with "the right not to be subject to a decision based solely on automated processing, including profiling, which produces legal effects concerning him or her or similarly significantly affects him or her automated individual decision-making, including profiling." If Article 22 of the GDPR adds the possibility for the data subject to consent to be submitted to profiling, this consent must be explicit and the data subject has "at least the right to obtain human intervention on the part of the controller, to express her or his point of view and to contest the decision." This is the main asset of the new regime of the regulation of profiling. It aims at giving the individual the possibility to protect himself from the above-mentioned phenomenon of the "algorithmic governability." Furthermore, the profiling based on sensitive data is prohibited as a principle in the last paragraph of Article 22.

Article 22 is a condensed version of the integrated vision of the European Data protection law. It combines the self-informational control, the risk-based approach and the fair processing obligation.

2. *The New Guaranties Introduced by the GDPR*

Profiling has been included in the new obligations of the Prior Data Protection Impact Assessment (here after PIA) of the data controller (Article 35). As mentioned before, it clearly relies on a risk-based approach of a data protection law oriented on compliance.

Companies or public authorities and bodies whose "core activities consist of processing operations; which by virtue of their nature, their scope, and/or their purposes, require regular and systematic monitoring of data subjects on a large scale will be obliged to designate a data protection officer" (herein after DPO) (Article 37). Although this provision does not explicitly refer to profiling, the idea of massive monitoring of data subjects should be applied to the digital actors whose core business activity is profiling, such as data brokers and digital platforms.

Data brokers are "companies that collect consumer's personal information and resell or share that information with others."[38] In its 2015 annual report, the CNIL established that the data brokers are not a clear legal category.[39] The annual report observed that there are two kinds of data brokers:

- Data brokers who are intermediaries between the holder of the data wishing to sell a copy to other firms and the firms that wish to acquire these data and
- Data brokers who are processing the aggregation and the data enrichment collected by partners, customers, or public register on behalf of their clients or for its own benefits.

Furthermore, this provision should include other digital actors like digital platforms. The concept of digital platforms hasn't been yet clearly legally defined. It comprises at least an "environment of applications," content-sharing sites like YouTube, digital market places such as Amazon, eBay and AirBnB. But the French Conseil d'Etat proposed a broader definition in order to include all websites that are "gateways" to accessing other content or serve to allow interaction socially with their peers. Under this definition search engines and social networks are part of the concept of digital platforms. The main feature of the digital platforms is their role as intermediaries. As such, digital platforms process a lot of personal data and monetize their activities by monitoring data subject. But, they not always act as data brokers according to the above-mentioned definition.

The introduction of the PIA obligation for actors whose core activities rely on profiling should be seen as an illustration of the risk-based approach vision of the data protection law. The same idea should be applied to the GDPR concerns about children. These concerns could impact the regulation of profiling. For instance, Recital 71 seems to exclude children from individuals' automated decision including profiling. Article 8 provides special protection for the children below the age of 16 in case of information services directly offered to them. The processing will be only lawful if the consent is given and authorised by the holder of the parental responsibility over the child. The provision should limit the possibility for a child to register in a social network that could apply profiling.

---

38. See Étude annuelle 2014—Le numérique et les droits fondamentaux, La Documentation française, Paris 2014, in particular p. 216. This definition is inspired by the French Conseil du Numérique report on Platform Neutrality: Building an open and sustainable digital environment June 2014.

39. CNIL "Data brokers: le pétrole et l'iceberg," annual Report 2015 p. 80.

The GRPD also provides reinforcement and harmonisation of sanctions in case of violation of the above mentioned Article 22, namely 20 000 000 € or 4% of the total worldwide annual turnover.

Those novelties could be appreciated in two ways. On the one hand, sanction should be seen as the failure of the regulation proposed by the DPAs. One the other hand, the novelties introduced by the GDPR relating to the sanctions will reinforce the power of incitation of the DPAs.

Last but not least, the GDPR clarifies the geographical scope of the European Data Protection law. Article 3§ 2 takes into account the fact that the data controllers operate in the digital/online market. First, it recalls that the GDPR should be applied in the context of the digital economy where the collection and the personal data processing are seen as the counterpart of free offering of goods and services like emails, social network accounts, etc. If it is free, it is because you are the product. Secondly, Article 3 § 2 considers that big controllers including data brokers, the GAFA, and cloud computing actors are mainly established outside the EU territory. So, Article 3§ 2 b) states that EU Data protection law applies on the monitoring of the personal data of individuals who are in the EU even if the data controller or processor is established outside the EU territory. This has been seen by certain scholars as the extraterritoriality effect of the EU law. However, such a point of view is not totally true.[40] The application of EU law is still related to the EU territory. The EU data protection law will only apply to the monitoring of the behaviour of the EU-located person, "as far as their behaviour takes place within the EU." Article 3 does not refer explicitly to profiling, but behavioural monitoring should be considered as the first step of the profiling process.[41] This particular issue has already been discussed in the *Google v. Spain* case and also in some cases involving Facebook.[42] In both cases, the ECJ has declared that the application of EU data protection is not submitted to the location of the data processing. Article 3 § 2 elucidates the criterion that has to be used to involve the non-EU actors. "So a U.S. ad network provider with U.S. corporate customers

40. To better understand what is really extraterritoriality, see Svantesson, D.J.B (2013). Extraterritoriality in Data Privacy Law. Copenhagen: Ex Tuto Publishing; Kuner, Christopher, Extraterritoriality and Regulation of International Data Transfers in EU Data Protection Law (August 30, 2015). Forthcoming in International Data Privacy Law, Volume 5, Issue 4 (2015); University of Cambridge Faculty of Law Research Paper No. 49/2015. Available at http://ssrn.com/abstract=2644237.

41. Recital 21 explicitly follows this interpretation.

42. ECJ 13 May 2015 Google Spain v. Costeja C-131/12, ECJ 6 October 2015, Schrems case C-362/14.

who wish to target ads and profile EU residents will be caught even though it has no physical presence in the EU."[43] Consequently, Article 3§4 should be relevant in the context of profiling.

In addition, the GDPR clarified that controllers and processors of personal data fall within its scope.[44] A data processor is an entity that processes the data on behalf of the data controller. The processor plays an important role, such as storing the personal data collected by the controller in the Cloud computing services. The GDPR will apply directly to processors and they are subject to direct legal obligations. As an example, they will have to show accountability. They will be directly responsible for data security, etc. They will also have to cooperate with DPAs that will have the power to investigate and to impose fines to processors. In the framework of the regulation, profiling will trigger the enforcement of the EU law, whether it is done by a EU processor or a non-EU based processor.

However, these applications of the European data protection law to non-EU actors has raised some difficulties in terms of effectiveness that will be addressed subsequently.

3. *The Improvement of Guaranties Relating to Fair-Processing Obligations*

Broadly speaking, the GDPR reinforces the obligation of transparency[45] and sets out new obligations of information relating to profiling. The GRPD forces the controller to inform the data subject of the existence of a profiling and information-collection scheme and about the consequences of this scheme. This rule applies whenever personal data is obtained from the data subject[46] or not.[47] Article 12 links this obligation to a combination of "standardised icons" that should provide "easily visible, intelligible and clearly legible" information. In addition, Article 15 grants a right of access to the information upon request to the data controller.[48] These provisions aim at giving the data subject elements for using other rights, like the right to object.

---

43. Victoria Hordern, The EU General Data protection regulation: A brave New world for processors, Bloomberg BNA, February 2016.

44. Ibidem.

45. Beatriz Tomàs Mallèn, Transparencia y protección de datos: nuevos desafíos para la garantía europea de los derechos fundamentales in Hacia un Nuevo Derecho Europeo de Datos, op.cit. p. 819.

46. Article 13 (f).

47. Article 14 (g).

48. Article 15 (h).

Article 21 outlines that the right to object can be used at any time for processing including profiling.[49] A special paragraph stresses that this right to object applies to processing in direct marketing. Recital 70 adds that the data subject has to be explicitly informed about his right to object. It means clear and separate information. Data subject should be able to exercise this right at any time and free of charge.

Beside the obligation of notification of data breaches to the DPAs, data controllers will also have the obligation of notifying individuals of the breach without undue delay if the breach is likely to result in a high risk for the individuals' rights and freedoms. This obligation will allow any data subject who has given his consent to profiling to be informed and to have the possibility of withdrawing his consent if he considers that the company has not taken sufficient security measures. The potential e-reputation damage of the disclosure of collected data used for profiling will encourage the controller's company to improve its security obligation. This should become a corporate social responsibility challenge.

§2 The Need for Improvements

The proposed European legal framework for profiling still has room for improvement. It should seek a more consistent and comprehensive approach based on the reality of the Big Data and smart technologies.

A. The Need for a More Consistent and Comprehensive Approach of Profiling Based on Big Data and Smart Technologies

1) The Ambiguities of the Harmonised Definition of Profiling

It is still ambiguous whether the definition of profiling really includes the creation and the application of profiles.[50] It would have been clearer if the definition had specified the different stages of profiling. It has been considered that profiling includes at least three steps: the collection of data; the creation

49. Article 21.1.

50. This concern has been expressed by DPAs. see G29 advice paper on essential elements of a definition and a provision on profiling within the EU General Data protection Regulation, Adopted on 13 May 2013p.2 and G29 Core topics in the view of the trilogue, 17 Junes 2015, p.14; The Belgian Commission pour la Protection la Vie Privée (CPVP) avis 23/2015 p.15, avis 10/2014 point 41.

of profiles; and the application of these profiles to individuals.[51] One could also regret that the core concepts of profiling have not been defined. A definition of the concept of profiles could have shown that the GPDR applies to the creation of profiles. Two indices could have been used in favour of this comprehensive interpretation. Firstly, profiling has been considered as a form of "processing" (which could rely on the construction of profiles) and to "analyse or predict aspects concerning" a person (meaning the application of profiles).[52] Secondly, it could explain why the definition of profiling does not mention the term of decision, although profiling is about decision-making by using or by applying profiles.

Furthermore, the GDPR clearly limits its scope to the profiling of personal data, unlike the European Council recommendation.[53] The collection and analysis of anonymous data (data mining) for the creation of a profile seems not to be considered. The processing of personal data often appears at the last stage of the inference, when the group profile is applied to an individual person.

The justification of the limitation of the definition of profiling to personal data could be linked to the scope of the RGDP. This may explain why it has not been criticised by the G29. Its proposed definition is also limited to the profiling of personal data. This difficulty had been seen in the explanatory memorandum of the Council of Europe recommendation. But the recommendation argues that "Profiling results in the creation of new personal data from anonymous data: both the warehoused data (which may be anonymous) that constitute the raw material and the process whereby the new data are created must be designed, and possibly adapted, so that the end result of the profiling process is personal data that are as accurate as possible, in accordance with Article 5.d of Convention No. 108. Since the quality of these two basic ingredients at the end of the profiling process is clearly of key impor-

51. See the recommendation of the Council of Europe point 38.

52. Sarah Johanna Eskens, op. cit p. 17.

53. The definition of profiling proposed by the Profiling project therefore underlined that "Profiling is a technique to automatically process personal and non-personal data, aimed at developing predictive knowledge from the data in the form of constructing profiles that can subsequently be applied as a basis for decision-making. A profile is a set of correlated data that represents a (human or non-human, individual or group) subject. Constructing profiles is the process of discovering unexpected patterns between data in large data sets that can be used to create profiles. Applying profiles is the process of identifying and representing a specific subject or to identify a subject as a member of a specific group or category and taking some form of decision based on this identification and representation."

tance in maximising the accuracy of the personal data generated, Article 5.d requires that all reasonable precautions should be taken to guarantee that quality."[54] In other words, the non-integration of a clear definition of profiles and the limitation of profiling on personal data put at risk the effectiveness of the definition.

At the end of the day, the proposed definition of profiling will face two difficulties: either be too broad, including all automated processing,[55] or be too restrictive, by not including the collection of all kinds of data (personal or not).

2) The Weaknesses of the Regime of Profiling

a) The Difficulties to See the Added Value of Article 22

Three factors make it difficult to see the real added value of Article 22. First, the wording of Article 22 § 1 is too complicated and ambiguous. The continuation of a negative approach of the proposed right raises questions about its nature. Having the right not to be subject to a decision on profiling could mean a prohibition of such processing or having a right to object to it. This second possibility has already been seen in the right to object under article 21 GDPR. So, if Article 22 could be seen as a special form of right to object, it should give more protection to the data subject than Article 21 does.

A comparative analysis of both rights does not enable to see what should be done. Article 21 sometimes seems to give more possibilities to the data subject because it includes the right to object to the decision not based solely on automated processing including profiling. One difficulty in profiling will be to prove that the profiling has led to an automated processing without any human intervention. In such circumstances, the use of the classic right to object will be useful, in particular if it is a processing scheme for direct marketing purposes. In such cases, the data subject benefits from a broad right to object that has not been submitted to the controversial balancing test with the legitimate interests of the controller. Furthermore, the result of the objection is the end of the processing for such direct marketing purpose. When it is not a processing scheme for marketing purposes, Article 21 still foresees the possibility for a data subject to object to the necessity of a processing scheme imposed by the data controller for two purposes—the performance of a task carried out in the public interest and the legitimate interests of the controller. The

---

54. See point 56.

55. See Christopher Kuner, Christopher Kuner, The European Commission's Proposed Data Protection Regulation: A Copernican Revolution in European Data Protection Law (Privacy and Security Law Report), Bloomberg BNA, 6 February 2012.

data subject will not have to prove anymore that he has "compelling legitimate grounds" to object. Nevertheless, the right to object should be exercised on grounds relating to the data subject's situation." The GDPR implies that there is a change in the burden of proof. It will be up to the controller to demonstrate that the processing should be maintained for compelling legitimate grounds.

The added value of Article 22 § 1 in comparison with Article 21 could be to create a real prohibition situation on decision solely based on automated profiling.

Secondly, if one agrees that Article 22 really provides a ban on profiling, the scope of this prohibition is ambiguous. In principle, Article 22 § 1 provides a ban of those kinds of decisions that could be overridden in three exceptions: necessity for the performance of the contract; legal authorization; and explicit consent of the data subject. Even, the prohibition of profiling of sensitive data can be overridden by the explicit consent of the data subject or a legal authorisation. This gives the impression that prohibition could become an exception. This also questions the application of the rule: exceptions to a principle must be strictly interpreted. Furthermore, the prohibition is limited to the decision based solely on automated decision of profiling "which produces legal effects concerning the data subject or similarly significantly affects him or her." Recital 71 gives only two illustrations of what that could be: "an automatic refusal of an online credit application or e-recruiting practices without any human intervention." In other words, it covers the exclusion of the service but we could also imagine a price discrimination based solely on a profiling mechanism of personal data.

Thirdly, the introduction of the possibility to override the prohibition by the data subject's explicit consent is ambivalent. On the one hand, it appears necessary because a lot of individual automated decisions based on the behaviour of the data subject are taken in the interest of the person. On the other hand, this consent-based approach does not seem to be appropriate for the smart technologies.[56] To what extent can this consent be explicit and informed in the smart environment, where people are always connected? Smart technologies often imply the absence of keyboards or monitors and a real time monitoring. In this environment, the informed and explicit consent could not rely on standard contract terms or icons.

56. See Sarah Johanna Eskens, op.cit. or Lilian Edwards, "Privacy, security and data protection in smart cities, a critical EU Law perspective, Create Working paper," 2015/11 december 2015; Natalie Helberger, Profiling and targeting consumers in the Internet of things A new challenge for consumer law?

b) *Maintaining Doubts about the Consent[57] Regulation*

Even aside from the smart environment, the place of consent in the European Data protection law is overestimated.[58] It has been demonstrated by behavioural sciences that people are used to agreeing to everything in order to access to services.[59] The relative success of the cookies legislation should be mentioned here. Most people click on the cookies banner without paying attention to what it means, maybe the same way that nobody reads completely the terms and conditions document of the digital services they use. In the praxis, two main difficulties have been seen. How to be sure that the data subject consents to all the purposes of the data controller and also to the second use of personal data? Under such context, the explicit consent condition introduced by the RGPD should not really improve the individual empowerment. Maybe, this is the paradox of the current priority given to the right of individual control in the European Data protection law. The consent is not really used with the purpose of giving more control to the data subject on his personal data. It is much more of a way to override the rights given to the data subject in order to facilitate the processing and the circulation of the data for the data controller.[60] Finally, the data subject control over his personal information seems to be much more of an illusion than a reality. Real protection should be sought, even in the presence of the people's consent.[61]

---

57. For a comprehensible analysis of the consent see Eleni Kosta, Consent in European in European data protection law, PhD thesis of the University of Leuven, Martinus Nijhoff Publisher 2013.

58. Many scholars have already questioned whether informed consent can be an effective measure of protection. Gabriela Zanfir, "Forgetting about consent: Why the focus should be on 'suitable safeguards' in data protection law?" Working paper May 2013 University of Craiova, Available at SSRN: http://ssrn.com/abstract=2261973, Daniel J. Solove, Privacy Self-Management and the Consent Dilemma, 126 Harv. L. Rev. 1880 (2013), Peter Blume, The inherent contradictions in data protection law, International Data Privacy Law 2012 p. 26–34.

59. F.J. Zuiderveen Borgesius, Improving privacy protection in the area of behavioural targeting, op. cit. p. 298.

60. Nicolas Ochoa, Pour en finir avec l'idée d'un droit de de propriété sur ses données personnelles: ce que cache véritablement le principe de libre disposition, RDFA 2015, p. 1157.

61. Frederik Johannes Zuiderveen Borgesius, Improving Privacy protection in the area of Behavioural Targeting, op.cit. in particular in chapter 9.

c) The Concerns about EU Law Enforcement on Non-EU Actors

Anu Bradford underlined the "Brussels effect."[62] This expression characterises "the unprecedented and deeply underestimated global power that the European Union is exercising through its legal institutions and standards, and how it successfully exports that influence to the rest of the world." In this article, Privacy Regulation is seen as an example of unilateral regulatory globalization.

It could be considered as legitimate that the European Data protection law applied to non-EU actors, but this would lead to difficulties. How the European actors could obtain the enforcement of those European obligations on non-EU actors? Dan Jerker B. Svantesson[63] is right when he recalls that targeting like the Article 3 of the GPDR is: "the legislator's dream and the judge's nightmare." He foresees that the proposed Regulation "bites off more than it can chew." In his opinion, "the actual enforcement will no doubt be concentrated on bigger actors having a substantial impact on the European market." However, the current difficulty for the French CNIL in imposing its global vision of the implementation of the de-listing right to Google is a good illustration of the difficulties in solving this kind of issues, even with big actors.[64]

A global legal framework for data protection is still needed as well as more international cooperation between the DPAs. Meanwhile, some practical solutions could be implementing in order to secure the international business of profiling. This business could partially take the form of transfers of personal data to third countries. It can be regulated by a decision of adequacy such as the Privacy Shield for the EU-US Data transfers. Binding corporate rules (BCR) and contractual clauses can also be used. Article 47 of the GDPR expressly imposes to include in the BCR the same guaranties as in Article 22 regarding profiling.

B. The Need to Improve the Effectiveness of the Regulation of Profiling

Finally, a compromise emerged after four years of negotiations on a harmonised definition. Yet, the legal regime for profiling still has many flaws, ambiguities and numerous exceptions.

---

62. Anu Bradford, "The Brussels Effect," Northwestern University Law Review, 2012?

63. Dan Jerker B Svantesson, extraterritoriality and targeting in EU data privacy law: the weak spot undermining the regulation, International Data privacy Law 2015 p. 226 sp.p. 232.

64. Olivia Tambou, Protection des données: la difficile mise en œuvre du droit européen au déréférencement, Revue Trimestrielle de Droit Européen, n°2 2016.

1) *Too Much Flexibility Left to the Member States*

The harmonised approach driven by the GDPR[65] provides a wide margin for manoeuvre for the Member States regarding two main issues. Article 8 should limit the possibility for a child to subscribe to a social network that could apply profiling. But after all, the GDPR through the National Law gives the possibility to introduce a lower age limit, provided that it is not below 13. Another important flexibility is given to the Member State in order to authorise a profiling mechanism, including the profiling of sensitive data. Article 22.4 only refers to the necessity of implementing "suitable measures to safeguard data subject's rights and freedom and legitimate interests." The Recital 71 gives some elements of these measures. It promotes the use of technical solutions, such as privacy by design, and certification.

2) *A Great Deal Remains to Be Done*

a) *In the Framework of the GDPR*

The effectivity of the protection of the data subject is based on the accountability principle of the data processor, as well as the controls and the coordination between the DPAs.[66] Those actors have two years to get ready for the coming implementation of the GDPR. It has already been planned that the European Data Protection Board (hereafter EDPB) should design some guidelines in order to specify "the criteria and the conditions for decisions based on profiling." The criteria and condition as are ones that could be authorized.[67] As mentioned before, the EDPB should also provide an opinion on the icons that could be used in order to ensure the transparency of the information, including for issues related to profiling.[68] At the end of the day, the implementation of such icons will need to be adopted by a delegated act of the European Commission.[69] The use of icons for privacy policies has been mainly limited to academic work. Various systems have already been imagined, inspired by the EU Energy

---

65. Olivia Tambou, Les enseignements de la réforme sur la protection des données personnelles au regard du concept d'harmonisation, in Harmonisation et Union européenne, to be published at the Revue de droit de l'Union européenne Mars 2017.

66. Olivia Tambou, "Remedies and European personal data protection law reform: what is new?" in *Comparative Perspectives on Remedies: Views from Four Continents* Russell L. Weaver, Arnaud Raynouard, Duncan Fairgrieve, Steven I Friedland (Eds), Carolina Academic Press, Forthcoming April 2017.

67. Article 70 (f).

68. Article 70 (r).

69. Article 12 §8 GPDR.

Label, the laundry labels, creative Commons, Platform for privacy Preference (P3P) etc.[70]

The GDPR also provides the creation by the EDPB of the European Data Protection Seal.[71] This European certification could include elements of privacy by design and by default which, could facilitate the regulation of profiling in smart environment.

b) *Beyond the framework of the GDPR*

Three other European issues should impact the legal framework relating to profiling. Firstly, the revision of the e-Privacy rules has been announced by the Commission when it had the Digital Single Market (DSM) Strategy on 6 May 2015. The e-Privacy Directive characterises and complements the Data Protection Directive 95/46/EC that will be replaced by the GDPR. Therefore, the public consultation opened on April 2016[72] contains several questions related to the interplay between the e-Privacy Directive and the future GDPR. This could be the right time to really engage and support a Do-Not-Track standard or a more effective tool[73] like a Do-Not-Target or a Do-Not-Collect, one with options for different kinds of commercial profiling. This could be inspired by the current Do-Not-Call list.

Secondly, the European Commission has organised a public consultation on online platforms. It covers the regulatory environment for online platforms, the liability of online intermediaries, data and the cloud, and the "collaborative economy." Until now, the Commission has only delivered the preliminary trends observed in this pubic consultation. "Most business and citizen respondents stated that platforms should be more transparent, notably about search results, clarity about the actual supplier and reviews mechanisms. They also consider that online platforms do not provide sufficient information on personal and non-personal data collected on their terms and conditions. The majority of citizen and online platforms who responded considered that the

---

70. Lilian Edwards, Wiebke Abel, *The Use of Privacy Icons and Standard Contract Terms of Generating Consumer Trust and Confidence in Digital Services*, CREATe Working Paper 2014/2015.

71. Article 42 GDPR, Olivia Tambou, L'introduction de la certification dans le règlement général de la protection des données personnelles: quelle valeur ajoutée? (The introduction of the Certification in the EU General Data Protection Regulation: What Added Value?), Available at SSRN: http://ssrn.com/abstract=2768093.

72. See Public consultation on the Evaluation and Review of the ePrivacy Directive.

73. Apparently the currently standard of Do Not Track does not block every tracking technologies.

above-mentioned problems consumers or suppliers perceive could be best addressed by a combination of regulatory solutions, self-regulatory and market dynamics. Responses from businesses were evenly divided between purely regulatory measures and a combination of market dynamics, self-regulatory and regulatory measures."[74]

Thirdly, a special reference should be made to the trade secret directive.[75] One of the main novelties of the GDPR is to include information and the transparency of the logic of the profiling. At the moment of writing this paper, it is not clear how this issue is intended to dovetail with the trade secrets directive.[76]

The necessity of consistency with the future regulation on e-privacy directive,[77] the adoption of the trade secrets directive and the expected issue of the new European Legal Framework on online Platforms on the platform[78] make it difficult to assess the real progress of the proposed European regulation of profiling.

Conclusion

This article has demonstrated that although the GDPR provides the first harmonised compelling definition of profiling, this definition and the proposed framework are not adapted to the realty of Big Data and the smart technologies. First of all, it is not fully clear whether the GRDP provides protection from both the creation of profiles and the application of profiles to an individual in case of solely automated decisions affecting him. Secondly, the GDPR does not take into account the creation of profiles based on anonymous data, which could also affect a data subject.[79] This observation is not called

---

74. European Commission; "First brief results of the public consultation on the regulatory environment for platforms, online intermediaries, data and cloud computing and the collaborative economy," January 2016.

75. Directive (EU) 2016/943 of the European Parliament and of the Council of 8 June 2016 on the protection of undisclosed know-how and business information (trade secrets) against their unlawful acquisition, use and disclosure, 0JEU L 157/1, 15/06.2016.

76. Gianclaudio Malgieri, *Trade Secrets v. Personal Data: a possible solution for balancing rights.*

77. The proposal for a regulation on Privacy and Electronic Communications, Com(2017) 10 Final from 10.01.2017.

78. See Communication on Online Platforms and the Digital Single Market Opportunities and Challenges for Europe COM(2016) 288 final.

79. See the recent study of Stanford computer scientists which show that telephone metadata can reveal surprisingly sensitive personal information, May 16, 2016.

into question by the new specification of the definition of personal data. In particular, this definition does not clearly include the concept of "singling out," which would allow a combination of metadata in order to characterise the behaviour of individuals.

Thus, the profiling issue should be seen as an illustration of the general criticism that one could use to address the GDPR. The ambiguous wording as well as the specification given only in the recitals, which in principle are not legally binding, and the flexibility left to the member States in important matters, augur that the GDPR will need a lot of interpreting, including on the judicial level.

Thirdly, this paper underlines that the GDPR proposed an integrated vision of the European data protection law based on three different approaches. The right-based approach of individual control of the data subject over personal data has been presented as the preferred approach. The risk-based regulation approach provides a complementary approach. It focuses on a scalable proportionate compliance taking into account when the processing is likely to result in a high risk to the rights and freedoms of a natural person. The fair processing obligations for the controller complete the European model of protection. The analysis of Article 22 shows that the principal added value of this article is to obtain human intervention on the side of the controller. This aims at giving the data subject the opportunity to express his point of view and the possibility to contest the solely automated-decision. The right to be informed about the logic and the consequences of the algorithms used for profiling are a step forward. However, these rights could be merely symbolic regarding the future trade secrets directive.

Finally, this paper questions the capacity of the current integrated vision of European data protection to really address the issue of profiling. The computing power of the algorithms makes it difficult to imagine how the explicit informed consent of the data subject could be implemented in order to enable real control by individuals of their personal data. The achievement of this unrealistic goal seems like carrying water in Danaïds' jars. The effectiveness of the legal framework of profiling would better be sought by a consistent approach on the impact of the Big Data and the smart technologies on profiling.

This might still be done through the coordination of the DPAs and the improvement of the European texts related to the European digital Market that are under discussion, such as the E-privacy Regulation, the trade secrets directive and the legal framework for the online platforms.